MW01170160

MEAN STREETS

A Journal of American Crime and Detective Fiction

Volume 2
Spring 2021

Copyright © 2021 by
Pace University Press
41 Park Row, 15th Floor
New York, NY 10038

ISSN 2691-6487
ISBN 978-1-935625-63-6

Member

Council of Editors of Learned Journals

♾™ The paper used in this publication meets the minimum
requirements of American National Standard for Information
Sciences—Permanence of Paper for printed Library Materials
ANSI Z39.48—1984

MEAN STREETS

EDITED BY
Rebecca Martin
Walter Raubicheck

Pace University
Pace University

MEAN STREETS

Co-Editors

Rebecca Martin
Pace University

Walter Raubicheck
Pace University

Editorial Board

Malcah Effron
Massachusetts Institute of Technology

Tonia Payne
Nassau Community College

Mary Rawlinson
SUNY Stony Brook

Roger Salerno
Pace University

Susan Elizabeth Sweeney
College of the Holy Cross

Samantha Walton
Bath Spa University, UK

MEAN STREETS

Volume 2, Spring 2021

Table of Contents

ESSAYS

APPRECIATION

REVIEWS

Editors' Introduction

Rebecca Martin and Walter Raubicheck

Ever since the publication of Edgar Allan Poe's "The Murders in the Rue Morgue" in 1841, the city has played a crucial role as the setting for modern crime fiction, especially by American authors. One thinks immediately of the San Francisco of Dashiell Hammett's Sam Spade, the Los Angeles of Raymond Chandler's Phillip Marlowe, and the New York of Rex Stout's Nero Wolfe. Hard-boiled crime fiction, in particular, has used the crowded city as the appropriate backdrop for its investigation of the ravages of greed and lust and used its labyrinthine streets as a metaphor for the complexity of its plots. This issue of *Mean Streets* is focused on the city, and especially New York, as it is used by American crime fiction authors in their most representative works.

Of course, American classical detective fiction authors also favored the city rather than the suburbs or the country as the logical setting for the crimes their detectives must solve. Think of the Philo Vance novels of S. S. Van Dine or the Henry Gamadge mysteries of Elizabeth Daly, the Ellery Queen novels of Frederic Dannay and Manfred Lee, and Stout's Nero Wolfe series (admittedly the wonderful hybrid of the classical and the hard-boiled). Though the classical British detective story has often favored the English country house for a setting, beginning with Wilkie Collins's *The Moonstone* (1868), the American version since Poe has always been closely allied to the urban environment.

In this issue of *Mean Streets*, New York is featured as both a site for crime fiction stories and as a center for the publishing industry. Firstly, Jennifer Nolan in "The Clues on the Cover: Scribner, P. D. James and the Making of a Literary Reputation" discusses the fascinating topic of how crime fiction is marketed vis a vis literary fiction, in particular how the copy on the book covers themselves demonstrates how the publisher views the author's work. The case in point here is P. D. James and the venerable New York house, Scribners, as the publisher gradually went from identifying her as an author of mysteries to including her works in their Paperback Fiction line along with Hemingway and Fitzgerald.

Nolan's analysis of the publishing industry's connection to the aesthetic quality of crime fiction is followed by four essays that use New York and its sister metropolis, London, and particular neighborhoods within the cities, as their settings for a range of thematic reasons. Antoine Dechêne in "From New York to Lyon and Back: Urban Detection in Paul Auster's *City of Glass* and René Belletto's *Eclipse*" stresses the alienation and loneliness of urban life and how they affect the detective in what he calls "metacognitive" mystery stories. In "Where Things Happen: Toxic Masculinity and Mike Hammer's New York City," Alexander N. Howe demonstrates how the diversity of New York only serves to form the basis of Mickey Spillane's detective's "racist, classist, and sexist" attitude towards his job. Joydeep Bhattacharyya then focuses on Harlem during the 1920s in the mystery novel by the Harlem Renaissance author Rudolph Fisher. Bhattacharyya sees the central conflict in the story to be the clash between mysticism and logic as investigative tools in "Harlem as the Confluence of Oriental Occultism and Western Rationalism in Rudolph Fisher's *The Conjure Man Dies: A Mystery Tale of Dark Harlem*." Finally, moving from the largest city in America to the largest city in Great Britain, Meghan P. Nolan analyzes the mysteries of *Bleak House* in "Institutional Paradox in the City: Duality, Domiciles and Death in Dickens's London."

Even one of our book reviews continues the urban theme as our reviewer evaluates a new book about Poe and the City, while our other review features a new book about the South in detective fiction, including film and television. Our Appreciation this issue is a tribute to M. K. Lorens and her series featuring the retired professor/author/detective Winston Marlow Sherman, who moves smoothly between an upstate college town and New York City.

From Nick and Nora Charles in *The Thin Man* to Dr. Laszlow Kreizler in Caleb Carr's *The Alienist* and Matthew Scudder in Lawrence Block's mystery series, American fictional detectives have emerged from the mean streets of New York as much as from those of any other American city, as this issue of our journal attests.

The Clues on the Cover: Scribner, P.D. James, and the Making of a Literary Reputation

Jennifer Nolan

Abstract

When thinking about American mystery and detective fiction, P.D. James, or rather Baroness James of Holland Park, is not generally the first—or hundredth—name that comes to mind. And nor, for that matter, is Charles Scribner's Sons, despite, or perhaps because of, their storied and important role in the history of American publishing more generally. Yet the story of how Scribners brought P.D. James's work to America is one that has much to reveal about how mystery and detective fiction has been defined, promoted, and understood in America throughout the latter half of the twentieth century and into the twenty-first.

From the initial US publication of P. D. James's first mystery, Cover Her Face, in 1966, the dust jackets and mass-market paperback editions of her works firmly positioned her as a genre fiction writer. However, in 2001, when Scribner made the choice to no longer option the mass-market paperback rights and instead bring out their backlist of her novels as trade paperbacks for the first time, they were visually and materially arguing that her work deserved to be in the same company as the literary classics that constituted that line, such as The Great Gatsby, to which the reprints bore striking similarities in all but one regard: each of the reprints of James's novels identifies her as a mystery writer multiple times. The covers' simultaneous similarities to literary fiction and repeated distinction of James as a mystery writer can be read both to reflect and to challenge cultural hierarchies that assert an inherent distinction between literature and mystery fiction. Unmasking the processes through which James's work was positioned and repositioned in the literary marketplace by Scribner(s) opens up larger questions about the flexibility and fixedness of genre boundaries and canon formation in America, and the role the paperback market plays in this process (as it had done many years before for another of Scribner's authors, F. Scott Fitzgerald).

In 2001, thirty-five years after publishing the first of P.D. James's novels in the United States, Charles Scribner's Sons withheld the paperback rights for their backlist of her novels from mass-market publishers and published them for the first time as trade paperbacks. Such a move was not unprecedented—indeed Scribners[1] entered the paperback business originally in the late 1950s when Charles Scribner, Jr., took back the rights to their literary titles, which had "been licensed to paperback and cheap-hardcover reprinters," and "invented the Scribner Library, [a] line of quality paperbacks" (Scribner, 1996 xxiii). The first in the Scribner Library series, a title now unequivocally considered a literary masterpiece, had itself just been through a twenty-year process of being resurrected from literary obscurity, and it was with this move that scholars generally agree that the novel's apotheosis (to use Charles Scribner III's term) was complete— coincidentally, like James's novel, also thirty-five years after its initial publication by Scribners. That book was F. Scott Fitzgerald's *The Great Gatsby*, and one of the most arresting things about the reprints of James's novels in 2001 is how much their covers mirror the cover of *Gatsby* in use at that time. With this move, Scribner[2] was visually and materially arguing that James's work deserved to be in the same company as such literary classics.

The story of how Scribners brought P.D. James's work to America reveals much about how mystery and detective fiction has been defined, promoted, and understood in America throughout the latter half of the twentieth century and into the twenty-first. From the initial

US publication of James's first mystery, *Cover Her Face*, in 1966, the dust jackets and mass-market paperback editions of her works firmly positioned her as a genre fiction writer. While the 2001 covers bear striking similarities to the covers of the literary works in the same line, they differ in one regard: each of the reprints of James's novels identifies her as a mystery writer multiple times. The covers' simultaneous similarities to literary fiction and repeated distinction of James as a mystery writer both reflect and challenge cultural hierarchies positing an inherent distinction between literature and mystery fiction. In "Laborers and Voyagers: From the Text to the Reader," Roger Chartier argues that "the transformation of forms and devices by which a text is presented authorizes new appropriations and consequently creates new publics for and uses of it" (56). Unmasking the processes through which James's work was positioned and repositioned in the American literary marketplace by Scribner(s) opens up larger questions about the flexibility and fixedness of genre boundaries and canon formation in America, and the role that publishers and the paperback market play in this process.

Coming to America:
P.D. James and Charles Scribner's Sons

Publishing P.D. James in the Scribner Paperback Fiction line in 2001 also placed her work in conversation with another famous contemporary of Fitzgerald's, Ernest Hemingway, whose works were published exclusively by Scribners in the United States for over ninety years, ending only when the copyrights began expiring in 2020.[3] As Robert Trogdon artfully explains in *The Lousy Racket: Hemingway, Scribners, and the Business of Literature*, "Hemingway's longest and most enduring relationship, lasting from 1926 to 1961, was with Charles Scribner's Sons" (12). In his conclusion, Trogdon argues that while equating "the development of an author's career and [their] reputation wholly to the influence of [their] publisher is misguided," studying the relationship between Hemingway and his publisher, Charles Scribner's Sons, is essential to understanding "how our perception of the writer and his work was shaped" (258). While the role played by Scribners in the trajectory of Hemingway's career was in many ways similar to the role that P.D. James's lifelong UK publisher, Faber & Faber, played in hers, in both cases American audiences' understanding of each author and their work was influenced and shaped by the publisher who brought their novels to the American market: Charles Scribner's Sons.

Among other similarities, both Hemingway and James developed personal relationships with more than one generation of the Scribner family that enriched and transcended their professional relationships. Charles Scribner, Jr., characterizes his father's relationship with Hemingway as "a close friendship" (Scribner, "Secret" 53), and described the "extraordinary warmth and kindness of [Hemingway's] letters" to himself (57), especially after his father's death. Scribner's description of his relationship with P.D. James, whose rights were purchased by Charles Scribner's Sons during his time as president of the company, is even more effusive. Beginning with their first meeting in 1968 after having published her first three novels in rapid succession, "no visit to England in later years was thinkable without an evening with Phyllis. We published her, of course, but seeing her was for pleasure. Conversation with her was entertainment in itself" (Scribner, *Company* 153). And she made an even deeper impression on his son Charles Scribner III: "She was, without question, my absolute favorite author I've ever gotten to know. There are very few authors, I have to say, that I would go to for help or advice, but I would go to her" (Scribner, personal interview). Such appreciation led Charles Scribner, Jr., to "bring her over to visit the United States in 1975," which in turn led to a "major media tour" two years later that "had a marked effect on her career and established her reputation in this country as a leader in her genre. . .as well as a novelist who transcended the genre" (Scribner, *Company* 153). Scribner's description here is revealing: not simply of his admiration for James, but also of how he felt about the status of mystery and detective fiction at the time.

When Charles Scribner's Sons introduced P.D. James to American audiences on July 7, 1966, with the hardback publication of her first novel, *Cover Her Face*, four years after it had been published in the UK by Faber & Faber, the dust jacket unequivocally indicated the genre and authors with whom they sought to position her work. As Gérard Genette explains in his foundational book *Paratexts*, literary works are surrounded by extratextual elements that provide an interpretation of the text to the reader. Of these, the publisher's paratext are those elements that are "the direct and principal . . . responsibility of the publisher," such as the covers, supplemental materials, and format (16). Genette cites "genre indications on some covers" as elements which can "make known an *intention*, or an *interpretation* by the author and/or the publisher" (11, emphasis in original), which is evident on Scribner's first edition of *Cover Her Face*. On the front cover, the book is described as "a mystery novel by P.D. James," while the back cover contains no information about James or the book and instead advertises other "leading crime writers from the Scribner list." The back flap features a photo and a blurb too brief even to be called a biography, saying only "this book introduces the talent of a fine new mystery writer who has finished a second novel and is at work on a third." Reading the cover, one sees clearly that what Scribners thought was most significant about this book for readers is the genre in which it belonged.

By 1975 when Scribners published her sixth novel, *The Black Tower*, the dust jacket included evidence suggesting that James was no longer an unfamiliar name to American mystery readers. As Scribners published each new book in the United States, her name became increasingly prominent on the cover, following Genette's basic precept that "the better known an author, the more space [their] name takes up" (39), and this front cover featured her name centered at the top in the largest font used to date. For the first time, the cover also identified the book as "An Adam Dalgliesh Mystery," a nod to the fact that this is the fifth in her long-running series featuring detective Dalgliesh and suggesting an assumed level of familiarity with this character as well. The back cover featured quotations from American and British reviews of James and her works rather than marketing her in relation to other mystery writers. And the back flap actually provided a few biographical details, along with information about her works and awards. Without question, however, like their edition of her first book, nine years later the paratext still firmly positions her as a crime writer. The biographical information tells us that she "works in the criminal department of the Home Office" and that her last two novels "have each won a Silver Dagger from the Crime Writers' Association in Great Britain and were runners-up for 'Edgars' from The Mystery Writers of America," and the quotations chosen from the reviews on the back emphasize her place among the great mystery writers, such as "Agatha Christie, Dorothy Sayers, and Ngaio Marsh."

The US paperback publishing history of James's novels provides more context for these shifts. After having appeared in hardback in the United States for nine years, beginning in the middle of 1975, Popular Library began to publish James's novels as mass-market paperbacks over a period of eighteen months. Despite Charles Scribner, Jr.'s well-known distaste for mass-market paperbacks, this lacuna between hardback and paperback publication was not due to his lack of trying to sell the paperback rights for her novels. Having come to somewhat of a detente with the paperback by this era, Scribner would license the paperback rights "whenever new bestsellers came out," saving only the literary classics for the Scribner Library (Scribner, interview). In particular, for years he'd attempted to interest Bantam, "the giant of paperback publishers in those days"[4] (Scribner, interview), in her works to no avail, despite being an (albeit reluctant) member of Bantam's board of directors since its creation in 1945.[5] As Charles Scribner III explained: "He sent copies [of her novels] to Oscar Dystel, head of Bantam books, and he said, 'Please, this is a great writer. Bring her out in Bantam books. You won't regret it.' And he never got a response."

When Popular Library was launched in late 1942, it focused primarily on mystery novels,[6] and it continued to be well known for its mystery authors even after expanding into other genres. By the 1970s, though not among the Big Five paperback houses, Popular Library had respectable sales, and they took care with James's first six novels in 1975, creating, in Charles Scribner III's estimation, "absolutely exquisite paperback covers, where each one was a shadow box with objects in it" depicting "elements of the novel" (interview).[7] Scribners was so pleased with the Popular Library editions, in fact, that they remained loyal to Popular Library when "every other paperback company wanted to buy [the rights] away" (Scribner, interview) after her popularity increased with the publication of her next two novels, *Death of an Expert Witness* (1977) and *Innocent Blood* (1980). In content, the mass-market covers published in 1975 are more similar to the Scribner edition of *The Black Tower* published earlier that year (and mentioned above) than to earlier Scribners hardback editions. Each of the books prominently features Antonia Fraser's assessment of James as "Agatha Christie's Crown Princess" centered at the top of the front cover, short quotations from reviews in popular American newspapers on both covers and within the book itself, and a biographical blurb on the back again telling us James works for "Britain's criminal department" and emphasizing her other books and her mystery-writing awards. Though the blurbs are a bit juicer and the quotations a bit shorter than those on the hardback versions, like the Scribners dust jackets, these covers provide no equivocation about how we are to view James – as an accomplished *mystery* writer.

P.D. James Trades Up

In contrast, when Scribners reissued all nine of their backlist of P.D. James novels as trade paperbacks in their Scribner Paperback Fiction line, they were placing her works in conversation with some of Scribner's most canonical literary authors, like F. Scott Fitzgerald and Ernest Hemingway, both of whom had been featured in Scribner's trade, or "quality," paperback series since the inception of the Scribner's Library in 1960.[8] Created initially for use in college classrooms,[9] "quality paperbacks sold at a higher price because they were not the usual small pocket books, but full-sized with good margins and good print" (Scribner, *Company* 108) in order to make reading and annotating easier. The association between the quality of the material book and the quality of the text became codified through their association with higher education, and throughout the twentieth century Scribner's living mystery authors were generally licensed to mass-market houses, as James had been, rather than published in their trade paperback lines. The Scribner Paperback Fiction line itself was launched in 1995 as "an independent series for classics and contemporary fiction" (Delaney 76) with preeminent Fitzgerald scholar Matthew J. Bruccoli's edition of *The Great Gatsby* making up one of its five initial titles. As Charles Scribner III explained, "it was something really new to have P.D. James join these classic authors":

> It was a big deal. And I thought, boy, has the wheel of fortune come full circle. Back in 1960, my father was launching Scribner Library paperbacks with their uniform gray covers, and here we are, forty years later, with P.D. James – our famous mystery novelist, not a classic author like Fitzgerald, Edith Wharton, Hemingway – being reclaimed and added to the Scribner paperback classics. I was delighted! (Scribner, interview)

In her extensive work on detective fiction, Erin Smith has noted that scholarly preoccupation with formulaic structures in the genre "ignores differences in the conditions of production and primary readership over time and in different media" and points out that "the 1920s and 1930s readers of Hammett in the cheap pulp magazine *Black Mask* are not the same readers (demographically speaking) who buy his novels in expensive Vintage Crime Classics paperbacks in 2000" (202-3). In much the same way, by retaining the paperback rights to P.D. James's novels and publishing them in their more expensive trade paperback line, Scribner was inviting different readers than those who enjoyed her work in mass-market paperback editions. While more concerned with variations in content and editorial procedure than in paratext, Michael Anesko's 2009 article in *Book History* on the collected editions of another writer with the last name James—in this case Henry—offers a useful way of thinking about different "so-called 'editions'": "as a particular event in the construction, marketing – and canonization – of the authorial phenomenon that we refer to as 'Henry James'" (188). The visual similarities between contemporary editions of uncontestably literary titles like *The Great Gatsby* or *The Sun Also Rises* and the reprints of P.D. James's novels are immediately and strikingly evident (see fig. 1), which are almost identical in terms of color and their placement of a central image, framed by the author's name at the top and the title of the book at the bottom. Like the names of Fitzgerald and Hemingway, the size and positioning of P.D. James's name at the top of the front cover suggest

Figure 1. Scribner Paperback Fiction: P.D. James *Cover Her Face* and F. Scott Fitzgerald *The Great Gatsby.*

that by 2001 Scribner felt comfortable relying upon "the authorial phenomenon" known as P.D. James to sell books, and that this edition is taking a step forward in her canonization. These similarities carry over to the back cover as well, where the formatting and color are again similar, as is the content. Each edition begins with a brief one-paragraph summary of the book, and both *Gatsby* and *Cover Her Face* end with one-sentence assertions of their value: "*The Great Gatsby* is one of the great classics of twentieth-century literature" and "*Cover Her Face* is P.D. James's electric debut novel, an ingeniously plotted mystery that immediately placed her among the masters of suspense." Likewise, the biographical statements following the summaries include assertions of each author's importance: "Fitzgerald stands out as one of the most important American writers of the twentieth century," "Ernest Hemingway did more to change the style of English prose than any other writer in the twentieth century," and

P.D. James is "widely acknowledged as 'the greatest contemporary writer of classic crime.'"

Yet one important distinction remains, which is evident in this final set of quotations. Each of the reprints of James's novels identifies her as a mystery writer multiple times. Though in smaller print than the rest of the text, each front cover includes a quotation from *Time* distinguishing James as "the reigning mistress of murder." On the other hand, the back cover is less circumspect about defining her this way. Directly under her name we're told that she "is the greatest living mystery writer," and the remainder of the text provides us with evidence to this effect through a list of her accomplishments as a writer of crime fiction and positions the particular book within this canon. Each back cover also identifies the book as a mystery in tiny font at the top right corner. Returning to Genette's analysis of the role of genre indications, it's clear that whatever else Scribner is intending, they are still suggesting that the reader interpret these books primarily as mystery novels.

The positioning of James between literary fiction and mystery fiction evident on the covers is also reflected in the way quotations from reviews are used to position James and her works. The opening page of each book contains "Praise" for both the book and P.D. James herself, which emphasizes a mixture of literary and mystery fiction traits. An excerpt from the *Christian Science Monitor* places her in conversation with literary greats: "One reads a P.D. James novel in something like the spirit that one reads a novel by Zola, Balzac, Thackeray, or Dickens." Another, from the more lowbrow *People* magazine, emphasizes qualities more traditionally associated with mystery fiction: "James delivers the pace and tensions of a mystery yarn better than any other living writer." And a third, from *Vogue*, places her in conversation with the best of the genre: "P.D. James ... writes the most lethal, erudite, people-complex novels of murder and detection since Michael Innes first began and Dorothy Sayers left us." As Elizabeth Long has noted in her influential work on Houston book clubs, the machinations of both the book and culture industries play an important, though largely invisible, role in framing how readers classify and evaluate books (117-8). One result of this is that these book groups, unless specifically created for readers of a particular genre, rarely read genre fiction, and mysteries are generally considered only slightly more acceptable than science fiction or romance novels (120). That said, "one reason that detective fiction outranks" other genres is its perceived association with "things literary," such as references to the classics, "word play," and "things British." Thus, authors like Dorothy Sayers, to whom James is compared in the *Vogue* quotation in the front of each Scribner's edition, are able to serve as "high quality exceptions within their humble genre" (129).

The roots of these biases in academic discourse are well-established, and these hierarchies still maintain such cultural authority in the United States that they even shaped the ways P.D. James and her work were discussed in the obituaries published upon her death in 2014. Writing for the *Washington Post*, Steve Donoghue began by deeming her "the British author whose cerebral murder mysteries brought a new level of sophistication to the genre," while Jill Lawless's obituary for the *Los Angeles Times* was titled "A Crime Writer Beyond Genre." Even more revealing was the obituary written for the *New York Times* by Marilyn Stasio, the *New York Times Book Review's* Crime columnist since 1988, who, having read "more than 150 crime novels a year" (Fromson 2), surely has few peers more familiar with the genre. While Stasio's obituary for the *New York Times* presented a more nuanced interpretation, acknowledging James's own discomfort with these types of comments—"reviewers frequently lauded Ms. James for 'transcending the genre,' but she was a champion of the detective mystery, which she called 'a literary celebration of order and reason'"—Stasio nonetheless reinforces the critical view that James rejects by claiming that James's books "elevated the literary status of the modern detective novel." What unifies all of these examples is the taken-for-granted assumption that mystery and detective fiction is of a lower quality and status than literary fiction—an assumption, it should be noted, that P.D. James frequently spoke out against.

According to James, this bias was especially strong in the United States. In an interview conducted in 1998 for American digital publication *Salon*, the interviewer, Jennifer Reese, begins the interview by observing that "just about every time [James's] name is mentioned, the question comes up about whether detective stories can be art," and asks James whether she is "sick of finding [her]self perpetually at the center of this debate." In response, James makes a point of emphasizing that this question seems especially pertinent in America, where "it does seem in the United States as if the mystery is a slightly despised form"—an assessment she makes just three years before Scribner's move to position her works alongside their literary classics.

As Joel Black explains in his 2010 article, "Crime Fiction and the Literary Canon," despite the relatively recent "canonization of crime literature," the literary academy still resists fully accepting mystery fiction as literature, and he anticipates that "a vigorous critical debate may be expected to continue concerning crime fiction's status as *high* literature or literary *art*" (76, emphasis in original). Evidence of the pervasiveness of this bias is clear in Doreen Saar's 2008 review of two books approaching detective fiction through an academic lens for the *Journal of Modern Literature*, which she begins by directly addressing the elephant in the room before examining the traditional exclusion of mystery and detective fiction from serious critical attention: "Writing about detective fiction for a respected literary journal would seem to put the reviewer in a position not unlike that of a detective investigating a murder in a well-regulated Stately Home: the murder is a fact, but it is an awkward fact" (150). Among detective writers she cites as challenging this "snobbery toward detective fiction" is P.D. James, who took up this topic directly in her 2009 nonfiction book *Talking About Detective Fiction*. In her introduction, James makes a compelling argument against those who dismiss mystery fiction on the basis of its formal structure by comparing it to one of the most rarified of poetic forms, the sonnet, a comparison which is worth quoting at length:

> One of the criticisms of the detective story is that this imposed pattern is mere formula writing, that it binds the novelist in a straitjacket which is inimical to the artistic freedom which is essential to creativity, and that subtlety of characterisation, a setting which comes alive for the reader and even credibility are sacrificed to the dominance of structure and plot. But what I find fascinating is the extraordinary variety of books and writers

which this so-called formula has been able to accommodate, and how many authors have found the detective
story liberating rather than inhibiting of their creative
imagination. To say that one cannot produce a good
novel within the discipline of a formal structure is as
foolish as to say that no sonnet can be great poetry since
a sonnet is restricted to fourteen lines—an octave and a
sestet—and a strict rhyming sequence. (10-11)

James, a well-known Janeite whose last published novel in 2011, *Death
Comes to Pemberley*, was a sequel to *Pride and Prejudice*, and who
also named her daughter after the author, then takes it a step further
and makes it clear that it's the writer, not the genre, that matters when
defining art: "All Jane Austen's novels have a common storyline: an
attractive and virtuous young woman surmounts difficulties to achieve
marriage to the man of her choice. This is the age-long convention of
the romantic novel, but with Jane Austen what we have is Mills & Boon
[the UK's top publisher of romance novels] written by a genius" (11).
Her well-earned defensiveness regarding the artistic status of mystery
fiction, and by extension her own work, is reflected both in these com-
parisons and in her tone, and, as Saar notes, this is a topic P.D. James
has been passionate about. As James notes in her autobiography *Time
to be in Earnest*, "Most aficionados of detective fiction would agree
with Chandler that his books should be read and judged not as escapist literature, but as works of art. I would only add that I don't see why
escapist literature shouldn't also be a work of art" (19).

Yet in the conclusion of *Talking about Detective Fiction*, James steps
back from this direct comparison with literature and instead seems to
assert a different role for genre fiction:

We do not expect popular literature to be great literature, but fiction which provides excitement, mystery
and humor also ministers to essential human needs. . .
[The] popularity [of the detective story] suggests that in
the twenty-first century, as in the past, many of us will
continue to turn for relief, entertainment and *mild intellectual challenge* to those *unpretentious* celebrations

> of reason and order in our increasingly complex and
> disorderly world. (195-196, my emphasis)

The shift from "great poetry" to "unpretentious celebrations" and "mild intellectual challenge" in just under 200 pages is striking, yet this inherent tension – if not contradiction – in James's own assessment of whether works of mystery fiction can be "great literature" seems to be reflected in the ways her mysteries were repackaged for the twenty-first century as well. While visually the covers align her work with the literary canon, textually, in their insistence on James as a crime writer, the covers can be read to position her outside of it. But do they?

One final paratextual feature of the Scribner's reprints further complicates this narrative: The Reading Group Guide at the back of each of their editions. While these sorts of guides are not traditionally included in editions of canonical novels, they emphasize tools commonly featured in literature classrooms such as close reading, examining authorial intention, and focusing on characterization. For example, the first question for *Cover Her Face* draws attention to James's characterization and technique by asking readers to look carefully at how she "convincingly" depicts the "murderer's state of mind without revealing the person's guilt." Another question gestures toward the social implications of James's choices in *A Mind to Murder* by asking the reader to consider "why James chooses to make suspects of ordinary people rather than the mentally ill," and many questions highlight character development through analyses of Dalgliesh's choices. By mimicking academic discourse in these questions, Scribner is telling readers that James can appropriately be read and evaluated in the same ways that more serious literature is discussed in the classroom, and explicitly invites them to do so. This also mirrors attempts by the mystery fiction reading groups in Elizabeth Long's study to "redefine mysteries as serious books" by "subjecting the books to the same process of categorization and evaluation that literary critics apply to the entire universe of literature" (126).

Just as P.D. James's comparison of the formulaic structure of mystery fiction to that of a sonnet belies arguments that posit an inherent distinction between mystery fiction and literature on the basis of form, paying attention to material differences in different editions of the "same" book belies assumptions that it is the text alone that determines its value and cultural significance. In his work on the popular publishing history of modernist writers, David Earle offers a useful way to think about these different, and sometimes contradictory, presentations of the (ostensibly) same text: "The marketing provenance of a book, its very materiality, constitutes a literature of its own, a constructed aura or psychology of the physical book that is symbiotic to the fiction as well as our understanding of it . . . given this, the dust covers of a Scribners first edition or a later Bantam paperback are each texts in themselves that tell very different stories" (158). Interestingly, in P.D. James's case, while the Scribners first edition and Popular Library mass-market paperback covers largely agreed in their unequivocal presentation of James as a mystery author, different and more complex stories were told when Scribner moved her novels into trade paperback. By placing James into the Scribner Paperback Fiction line with writers like Fitzgerald and Hemingway in 2001, Scribner was suggesting new reading protocols for her work and attempting to broaden the audience who read and appreciated her novels. Examining the role Scribner played in the shifting material presentation of James's works in the United States offers insight into the complex processes by which taste is generated, genre is defined, and cultural hierarchies are both challenged and maintained.

NOTES

The author would like to thank Charles Scribner III for his kindness, enthusiasm, and expertise, which was indispensable for bringing this project into its final form. She is also indebted to the Barzun-Taylor Mystery-Detective Collection at UNC libraries for their collection of different editions of P.D. James's novels. Those directly analyzed in the text of this article have been listed in the Works Cited, but examination of all first edition Scribners hardback, 2001 Scribner trade paperbacks, and 1970s Popular Library mass-market paperback editions underlies and informs my work. A much earlier version of this research was presented at the Society for the History of Authorship, Reading, and Publishing (SHARP) 2016 annual conference in Paris, France.

1. Though it changed from an independent company to an imprint through various mergers between 1978 and 1984, Charles Scribner's Sons was commonly referred to as Scribners throughout most of the period this article concerns, a shorthand I will employ here as well. In 1994, the "s" was officially dropped under Simon & Schuster,

thus references to the imprint after that date are written as Scribner (See Delaney's "Scribner Chronology" 71-76).

2. See note 1.
3. For more on the longevity of their relationship, see Trogdon, "Epilogue" and Scribner "My Life with Hemingway," *In the Company of Writers* 63-86.
4. See Davis 341-356 for more on Bantam's dominance of the market through the late 1970s.
5. Bantam was created by combining the might of several major players in the publishing world, including Scribner (Davis 103).
6. Indeed, all ten of the books in their first list were mysteries (Davis 95).
7. Interestingly, while the US printing of her work in hardback mirrored the order of their release in England, the publication order of the mass-market paperback reprints contrasted with the original publication order of the books, despite five of the six belonging to the Dalgliesh series. Thus, new readers would have had access to paperbacks containing the third, *Unnatural Causes* (September 1975), fourth, *Shroud for a Nightingale* (June 1976), and fifth, *The Black Tower* (August 1976), books in the Dalgliesh series, before the publication of the second, *A Mind to Murder* (October 1976), and finally the first, *Cover Her Face* (December 1976).
8. Fitzgerald's *The Great Gatsby* and *Tender is the Night* were featured as the first and second in the Scribner Library series, while Hemingway's *For Whom the Bell Tolls* and *The Sun Also Rises* were number four and five.
9. For an overview of the inspiration for and creation of quality or trade paperbacks for use in college, see Barnhisel 160-9. However, while the quality and sophistication surpassed that of mass-market paperbacks when they were first launched in 1953, the full-size used by the Scribner Library was an innovation of the later 1950s.

WORKS CITED

Anesko, Michael. "Collected Editions and the Consolidation of Cultural Authority." *Book History*, vol. 12, 2009, pp. 186-208.

Barnhisel, Greg. *James Laughlin, New Directions, and the Remaking of Ezra Pound*. UMass Press, 2005.

Black, Joel. "Crime Fiction and the Literary Canon." *A Companion to Crime Fiction*, edited by Charles J. Rzepka and Lee Horsley, Wiley-Blackwell, 2010, pp. 76-89.

Bruccoli, Matthew J., ed. F. Scott Fitzgerald's *The Great Gatsby: A Literary Reference*. Carroll & Graf, 2002.

Chartier, Roger. "Laborers and Voyagers: From the Text to the Reader." *Diacritics*, vol. 22, no. 2, Summer 1992, pp. 49-61. *JSTOR*, jstor.org/stable/465279.

Davis, Kenneth. *Two-Bit Culture: The Paperbacking of America*. Houghton Mifflin, 1984.

Delaney, John, ed. *The Company of Writers: Charles Scribner's Sons, 1849-1996*. Princeton Library, 1996.

Donoghue, Steve. "P.D. James, who brought a gritty realism to the British detective novel, dies at 94." Washington Post, 27 November 2014. wapo.st/1vRuuH8?tid=ss_mail.

Earle, David M. *Re-Covering Modernism: Pulp, Paperbacks, and the Prejudice of Form*. Ashgate, 2009.

Fitzgerald, F. Scott. *The Great Gatsby*, edited by Matthew J. Bruccoli, Scribner, 1995.

Fromson, Daniel. "Revered and Feared in the Book Review." *New York Times*, 25 June 2017, p. 2.

Genette, Gérard. Paratexts: *Thresholds of Interpretation*, translated by Jane E. Lewin, Cambridge UP, 1997.

Hemingway, Ernest. *The Sun Also Rises*. Scribner, 1995.

James, P.D. *The Black Tower*. Charles Scribner's Sons, 1975.

——. *The Black Tower*. Scribner, 2001.

——. *Cover Her Face*. Charles Scribner's Sons, 1966.

——. *Cover Her Face*. Popular Library, 1976.

——. *Cover Her Face*. Scribner, 2001.

——. *Talking About Detective Fiction*. Vintage, 2009.

——. *Time to be in Earnest: A Fragment of Autobiography*. Ballantine, 1999.

Lawless, Jill. "A Crime Writer Beyond Genre." *Los Angeles Times*, 28 Nov 2014, p. AA6.

Long, Elizabeth. *Book Clubs: Women and the Uses of Reading in Everyday Life*. Chicago UP, 2003.

Reese, Jennifer. "The Salon Interview – P.D. James." *Salon.com*, 26 February 1998. *NexisLexis*, advance-lexis-com/prox/lib.ncsu.edu/api/document?collection=news&id=urn:contentItem:4320-21F0-0103-S26D-00000-00&context=1516831.

Saar, Doreen Alvarez. "Writing Murder: Who is the Guilty Party?" *Journal of Modern Literature*, vol. 31, no. 3, Spring 2008, pp. 150-8. *Project Muse*, muse.jhu.edu/article/239933.

Scribner, Charles, Jr. *In the Company of Writers: A Life in Publishing*. Scribners, 1991.

——. "The Secret of Being Ernest (and the Secret of Keeping Ernest)." *In the Web of Ideas: The Education of a Publisher*, Scribners, 1993, pp. 35-62.

Scribner, Charles III. Personal interview. Conducted by Jennifer Nolan, 14 December 2020.

——. Preface. *Of Making Many Books: A Hundred Years of Reading, Writing, and Publishing*, by Roger Burlingame, Penn State UP, 1996, pp. vii-xxvi.

Smith, Erin. "Women's Hard-Boiled Detective Fiction." *Reading Sites: Social Difference and Reader Response*, edited by Patrocinio Schweickart and Elizabeth Flynn, MLA, 2004, pp. 189-220.

Stasio, Marilyn. "P.D. James, Creator of the Adam Dalgliesh Mysteries, Dies at 94." *New York Times*, 27 Nov. 2014, p. B11.

Trogdon, Robert. *The Lousy Racket: Hemingway, Scribners, and the Business of Literature*. Kent State UP, 2013.

From New York to Lyon and Back: Urban Detection in Paul Auster's *City of Glass* and René Belletto's *Eclipse*

Antoine Dechêne

Abstract

The city is the scenery of most metaphysical detective stories, a genre defined by the blurred distinction between the roles of the detective, the criminal, and the victim as well as by a crucial absence of closure. In such stories, the investigator loses his identity engulfed by the crowd and the city speed. From Poe's famous "Man of the Crowd" (1840) to Auster's characters in *The New York Trilogy* (1990), these urban detectives keep losing themselves as they long for ontological stability.

The city of Lyon in René Belletto's *L'Enfer* (1986, *Eclipse* in English) presents a different scenery in which the amateur sleuth does not suffer from alienation in the midst of the multitude, but from extreme solitude in a deserted city under the hellish sun of August. Belletto's detective, on the verge of committing suicide, is condemned to painful introspection when a wrong telephone number, just like in Auster's *City of Glass*, sets him in motion and urges him to roam through the streets and neighborhoods he knows so well.

In this context, this paper offers a comparative reading of Auster's first and Belletto's third novel in which the cities of New York and Lyon remind one of Walter Benjamin's foundational remark that "[t]he original social content of the detective story was the obliteration of the individual's traces in the big-city crowd" (Benjamin 43) while also revealing that extreme solitude can as well be a traumatizing experience that "eclipses" the detective in search of his own identity.

Auster and Belletto

This article proposes a comparative reading of two writers who wrote groundbreaking detective fiction parodies in the late 1980s: Paul Auster and René Belletto. While Auster's fiction has been thoroughly translated and studied, Belletto's work has barely been addressed by critics and even less by academics. Yet, a comparative analysis of Auster's and Belletto's fiction helps shed a different light on the former's much analyzed work. Indeed, both writers have many things in common. They are from the same generation: Belletto was born in 1945 and Auster in 1947. Both set most of their stories in the cities they grew up in: New York for Auster and Lyon for Belletto. Both are also poets, essayists, and short story writers. Both have published extensively and keep writing to this day. But most of all, both are the authors of two provocative detective fiction trilogies published exactly at the same time: while Auster was writing *City of Glass* (1985), *Ghosts* (1986), and *The Locked Room* (1986), published together as *The New York Trilogy* in 1987, Belletto was creating *Le Revenant* (1981), *Sur la terre comme au ciel* (1982), and *L'Enfer* (1986, translated into English in 1990 as *Eclipse* by Jeremy Leggatt). Although never gathered in a single volume, these novels are today known as the "Trilogie Lyonnaise" because the three novels are mainly set in Lyon and share hypertextual references in the same way the narrator of *The Locked Room* comments on the rest of the trilogy.

Both trilogies explore the genre of detective fiction by humorously subverting its codes and structures. What is more, both can be (and have been) studied through the lens of a genre called the metaphysical detective story, especially by focusing on the motif of the city, which emphasizes the sublime emptiness and loneliness characterizing the detective's impossible quests for (self-)knowledge and stable identity. Auster's first novel, *City of Glass*, and Belletto's concluding one, which is also his most famous and only translated one,

Eclipse, are the two texts which have most in common and will thus provide the basic material for this paper's close readings. After a brief detour to specify what is meant by metaphysical detective story, the article will move on to address the specific ways in which the urban settings of New York and Lyon determine, or rather, undermine the amateur sleuths' investigations. Both Auster's and Belletto's protagonists are writers who fail to describe their urban experience with the appropriate words. The paper will finally reflect on the different forms of solitude experienced by these two men who defy common sense by following their mad intuitions only to get lost trying to give some meaning to what their quest has become.

Metaphysical Detective Trilogies

What is a metaphysical detective story? The phrase is first coined by Howard Haycraft in 1942 to describe Chesterton's Father Brown tales. The critic conceives the metaphysical detective story as a distinct genre "chiefly concerned with the moral and religious aspects of crimes" (76). He calls the priest-detective's method "metaphysical" because it is based on an unexplainable intuition and an acquaintance with human nature rather than on reasonable deductions made after the discovery of physical evidence. If Dupin's method consists in identifying himself with his opponent, Father Brown trusts his ability to morally relate to the pursued felon and spiritually explain his propensity to evil.[1]

The phrase is then used in the seventies by Michael Holquist to characterize a literary subgenre closely related to the advent of postmodernism. Such a definition of the genre is based on a preconception of the "traditional" detective story as a highly structured and closed preexisting type of fiction that the postmodern "avant-garde" has been playfully subverting. For Holquist, alternative detective stories by Robbe-Grillet or Borges, for instance, "depend on the audience's familiarity with the conventions of the detective story to provide the subtext they may then play with by defeating expectations" (155). Yet, their metaphysical aspect does not rely only on the intertextual game they play with their readers in order to deceive them;

they are also concerned with the impossibility of building reliable knowledge. Holquist thus defines the metaphysical detective story as a kind of text which is "non-teleological, is not concerned to have a neat ending in which all the questions are answered, and which can therefore be forgotten" (153). Closure is one of the main features of the classical detective story, and, therefore, it only seems logical that the metaphysical genre – when understood as an exercise in subverting its predecessor– would undermine this need for *dénouement* by frustrating the reader's expectations.

The introductory chapter to Merivale and Sweeney's *Detecting Texts: The Metaphysical Detective Story from Poe to Postmodernism* (1999) is a foundational text in which the metaphysical detective story is described as "a genre of largely twentieth-century experimental fiction" (1), a genre which raises questions about "narrative, interpretation, subjectivity, the nature of reality, and the limits of knowledge" (1).

Merivale and Sweeney provide a very precise definition of the metaphysical detective story:

> A metaphysical detective story is a text that parodies or subverts traditional detective-story conventions – such as narrative closure and the detective's role as surrogate reader – with the intention, or at least the effect, of asking questions about the mysteries of being and knowing which transcend the mere machination of the mystery plot. Metaphysical detective stories often emphasize this transcendence, moreover, by becoming self-reflexive (that is, by representing allegorically the text's own processes of composition). (2)

This definition points at a number of very relevant features of the genre such as its highly intertextual and metatextual nature, its proximity with parody, its narrative unreliability, and its fundamental absence of closure, which has a very unsettling effect on readers, forcing them to a double questioning that goes beyond modernist versus postmodernist distinctions to an obsessive interest in both epistemological and ontological problems.

From this perspective, I have also pleaded for a shift in terminology between "metaphysical detective story" and "metacognitive mystery tale" (Dechêne). The phrase metacognitive mystery tale wants to account for (1) the cognitive questions on which those investigations are based and (2) the recurrent absence of professional detectives to lead these investigations. The term "metacognitive" is preferred to the more ambiguous "metaphysical" because it rejects Haycraft's use of the term to describe detective fiction that provides a religious or teleological explanation to life's mysteries. The metacognitive dimension of Auster's and Belletto's trilogies lies in their ability to question the possibility of indisputable knowledge while also alluding to the idea that meaning is a human construct, whose flaws and profound gaps can best be described through the concept of the sublime. Similarly, the phrase "mystery tale" is preferred to the too restrictive notion of "detective story," which implies a professional investigator and a need for resolution.

The city is the space where the metacognitive sleuths roam and feel, as Baudelaire famously wrote, "anywhere out of the world." Auster's and Belletto's detectives indeed seem to have things in common with the figure of the *flâneur* who, in mid-nineteenth century Paris, has become, in Benjamin's words, "an unwilling detective" (40). As he walks each day a little faster, the *flâneur* foresees that every step he takes "will lead him to a crime" (41). The detective wants to impose rational thinking while the *flâneur* is simply overwhelmed by the surplus of interpretative possibilities that lies behind each "countenance" of the city crowd. It is not a coincidence if the detective story develops in the human flux of city masses. As many critics have recalled, crime itself has often been apprehended as "a consequence of urbanization and the concomitant proximity of rich and poor within the confines of urban spaces" (Worthington 30) and thus the space of the city is the "privileged locale for crime fiction" (Schmid 14). It is precisely the multitude that frightens because it swallows the individual who seems to lose his own identity. Accordingly, for Benjamin, "The original social content of the detective story [is] the obliteration of the individual's traces in the big-city crowd" (Benjamin 43). The self disappears in such an incoherent mass and the *flâneur* "cease[s] to be [at] home" (47) in the city. He has lost his power to read and interpret the crowd, an outcome that Poe already envisioned in his foundational story "The Man of the Crowd" (1840).

Similarly, the metaphysical or metacognitive investigator does not have the confidence or intelligence attributed to characters like Dupin or Poirot. Rather, he exhibits the doubts and fears of his time, revealing that meaning is essentially arbitrary. No truths or firm knowledge can be found in the world, and this is what the *flâneur*, the initial "man of the crowd," figures out: his mystery "does not permit itself to be read" (475). Impersonated by characters such as Robbe-Grillet's Wallas in *The Erasers*, to give another example, the image of the *flâneur* perfectly matches the description made of a typical postmodern detective. Indeed, Wallas, in distinct "man of the crowd" fashion, "spends much of his time walking in circles through city streets, adopting roles for himself to boost his confidence or stepping into roles suggested for him by others, acting like a suspect before he is one, excusing his guilt before he becomes guilty" (Ewert 185). He embodies the role of detective, criminal, and victim in one.

Michel Soler in Belletto's *Eclipse* also corresponds to this characterization, with one big difference, however: the city of Lyon that he haunts like a ghost is not crowded but totally empty. The plot of Belletto's novel is somewhat hard to summarize in a few words. Michel Soler, the first-person narrator and protagonist, tries to do so himself towards the middle of the book, emphasizing the apparent randomness and lack of verisimilitude of his adventure:

> In a few days, in this dead city where it seemed impossible that anything could happen, where heat and the absence of people seemed to obviate all possibility of events, well, heat and the absence of people had produced very different results, in a week, seven days, I had passed myself off with persons unknown as a kidnapper and professional killer and had received a down payment of five thousand dollars, I had committed suicide, I had conducted several interviews with an internationally famous pianist, kidnapped a child, held the sister of this child prisoner with the intention more

or less of raping her, buried my mother, who had been slain in effect by one of the true kidnappers, shared a few days of perfect love with the sister [...], the child had been kidnapped from the first kidnapper by a second kidnapper, who had killed the detective who had just killed the first kidnapper, and wounded me [...] in a Renaissance townhouse in Old Lyon of which there is a replica in Berlin, an identical building in which three years ago the same child had already been held against his will, along with his father, and where the internationally renowned pianist I mentioned earlier... .(206)

One can directly grasp some of the leitmotiv of the story such as the role taken on by the fake detective, himself not deprived of a criminal instinct and also the victim of a machinery in which he seems to be trapped, the effect of loop triggered by the repetitive kidnappings, the omnipresence of doubles, etc.

What is even more fascinating is that everything started with a wrong telephone number: "'Hôtel des Étrangers?' said a man's voice. Wrong number. It wasn't the first time. The two numbers were similar, almost identical in fact" (24). This passage of course recalls a similar one in Auster's *City of Glass*:

It was a wrong number that started it, the telephone ringing three times in the dead of night, and the voice on the other end asking for someone he was not. Much later, when he was able to think about the things that happened to him, he would conclude that *nothing was real except chance.* (3)

Belletto and Auster were writing at the same time. Again, *L'Enfer* was published in 1986 and *City of Glass* in 1985. There is certainly a form of *Zeitgeist* going on here, since the two writers did not read or know about each other and yet proposed groundbreaking parodies of detective fictions, both beginning with wrong telephone calls to which bored and purposeless men answer, taking on the identity of someone they are not.[2]

Perhaps the two authors had the same source of inspiration. Indeed, *The Erasers* already has detective, Wallas, brought into a case because of a similar mistake: "following an error of the same kind: he had dialed the wrong number, and immediately events had followed one another so quickly that he had not been able to disengage himself; one thing led to another …" (Robbe-Grillet 336). For these writers, the telephone error seems to represent a form of pure chance that triggers their narrative plots. The miscommunication somehow encourages the protagonist to act randomly, thereby also creating the very case they are about to investigate.

Writing (in) the City

Another interesting point is that both Michel Soler and Daniel Quinn are writers who struggle to write. Michel wrote one book, *On Bach's Fugues* (1969), of which there is a single copy left: "I had of course wanted it to appear, but at the same time wanted it to vanish forever from the face of the planet" (Belletto 18). When he accepts to write the biography of the famous pianist, Rainer von Gottardt, he discovers that writing has become a most difficult task for him: "I was writing, but badly. I mean the handwriting. I was having trouble with the act of writing, almost sticking my tongue out like a schoolboy" (84). The sleuth's incapacity to write, his inability to interpret the clues and translate them into a pattern of coherent reasoning, appears as a determinant chronotope of the metacognitive mystery tale, synthetizing the unreadability of the mystery.

The same deficit in meaning can be found in *City of Glass*, which epitomizes the concept of the city as a text, highlighting the central motifs of walking and writing and the way these two activities are interwoven. For Quinn, the detective-writer, writing and walking, interpretation and pursuit, are identical activities that involve the deciphering of "urban hieroglyphics" (Marcus 248). Quinn's tail job echoes the pursuit of "The Man of the Crowd" and shows that writing and walking at the same time is a difficult task:

> For walking and writing were not easily compatible ac-
> tivities. If for the past five years Quinn had spent his
> days doing the one and the other, now he was trying to
> do them both at the same time. In the beginning he did
> many mistakes. It was especially difficult to write with-
> out looking at the page, and he often discovered that he
> had written two or even three lines on top of each other,
> producing a jumbled, illegible palimpsest. (76)

This pursuit makes Quinn reflect upon the possible meanings of
the "urban text" he is writing while walking. He wonders "what the
map would look like of all the steps he had taken in his life and what
word it would spell" (155), which amounts to say that Quinn has
psycho-geographical intentions: he wants to find meaning in his
wanderings. For now, he tries to map his itineraries as he follows the
old man, drawing shapes in his red notebook that strangely resemble
alphabetical letters. Quinn, in the traditional detective fashion, craves
to discover a clue "no matter how obscure" (83) and thus chooses to
believe that Stillman's actions are not entirely governed by chance.
He transcribes Stillman's steps into diagrams, forming the shapes of
the letters OWEROFBAB. Quinn completes this message as THE
TOWER OF BABEL, "conjuring up the Biblical narrative of the fall
into linguistic multiplicity which underlies Stillman's belief in a single
'natural' language of humanity" (Marcus 260).

Quinn uses the map as a tool liable to "rationaliz[e] and deraci-
nat[e] space in order to master it" (Alford "Spaced-out" 627). What he
fails to understand, however, is that "the mapper must remain station-
ary, must stay 'home' to understand the movement of the pedestrian
other" ("Spaced-out" 627). Such a map brings an "illusion of knowledge" ("Spaced-out" 627) which is soon undermined because Quinn,
like any metacognitive sleuth, does not "stay home," and in fact does
not even have a "home." By becoming a pedestrian, Quinn gains
perspective and even seems to find a proper language to describe his
urban experience, a hope which soon proves to be another sham:

> Then doubts came, as if on command, filling his head
> with mocking, sing-song voices. He had imagined the

whole thing. The letters were not letters at all. He had
seen them only because he had wanted to see them.
And even if the diagrams did form letters, it was only
a fluke. Stillman had nothing to do with it. It was all an
accident, a hoax he had perpetrated on himself. (86)

For a long time, however, Quinn truly believed in the power of
the sleuth to read and interpret the ontological and epistemological
contingencies of the world. In a very "conventional" way, he thought
that "[t]he detective is one who looks, who listens, who moves
through this morass of objects and events in search of the thought,
the idea that will pull all these things together and make sense of
them. In effect, the writer and the detective are interchangeable" (9).
The traditional detection method, Poe's "ratiocination," is one that
implies a perfect convergence of language and reality, in which signifiers and signifieds connect clearly and deliver a transparent, empirically verifiable narrative. This method is bound to fail in the context
of the definitions of the metacognitive mystery tale considered so
far. In fact, as Mathias Kugler has argued, "none of the detectives and
pursuers of clues in the trilogy succeed in combining signifier and
signified to a meaningful shape" because "[w]ords cannot convey
presence, reality or absolute truth" (102).

Quinn must realize that he knows nothing and that "nothing [is]
real except chance" (3). He feels trapped inside a "city of glass" that
does not bring transparency but reflection; a city of mirrors and doubles, a labyrinthine city of words in which signifiers can only refer
to other signifiers, thereby precluding the production of meaningful
information. As already suggested, New York symbolizes an inde-
cipherable grid where the psycho-geographer drifts in order to find
a place where the only new space he manages to get at is a liminal
"nowhere":

New York was an inexhaustible space, a labyrinth of
endless steps, and no matter how far he walked, no
matter how well he came to know its neighborhoods
and streets, it always left him with the feeling of being
lost. Lost, not only in the city, but within himself as

well. [...] On his best walks, he was able to feel that he
was nowhere. (4)

Richard Swope links Quinn's ability to lose himself with Hawthorne's
Wakefield story about a man who all of a sudden makes the in-
comprehensible decision to leave his wife and family. This is "made
possible," he explains, because both characters are convinced that
they can "always return home," a certainty that, as Swope concludes,
"is eventually stripped away" from Auster's amateur detectives (4).
"Wakefield" indeed works as a clear *mise en abyme* in the three short
novels of the *Trilogy*. As one of the most disturbing examples of a
missing person story, Hawthorne's tale epitomizes "the possibility of
losing one's position in the world" (5). If Wakefield eventually returns
to his basically unchanged home after twenty years, things happen
to be much more complicated for Quinn who, from the start, has
lost his son and wife and literally becomes homeless as his obsessive
investigation consumes him.

Walking through the grid of New York, Quinn seems to exist
outside space and time, to melt into the walls of the city that have
and will exist without him (139). By trying to impose order on the
urban chaos, Quinn has reached the "end of himself" (Shiloh 53).
Again, the ambivalent and highly complicated task of interpretation
is represented by the city itself which, as already observed, shares the
inherent ambiguity of the labyrinth:

> [I]n Auster's New York, gridded numbered streets and
> avenues appear constructed on rigorous mathematic
> principles. At first these seem to bear little resemblance
> to Auster's aimless peripatetic heroes. Yet as the tales
> unravel, differences turn out to be largely illusory. The
> city, for all its extended symmetries, is as mysterious and
> improbable as any western wilderness. (Margolies 158)

The city shapes and mirrors the mystery of the metacognitive mystery tale. It works as a *mise en abyme* of the process of cognition,
which consists in trying to impose order and meaning onto the
arbitrariness of signs surrounding the detective. The apparent sym-

metries which characterize the material and architectural urban environment are illusions which mask the fact that "there is nothing to be learned from the great world of New York other than that design only serves to conceal underlying disorder" (159).

As the paragon of postmodern cities, New York's conception as a "city of glass" indicates that it is made of surfaces. Once those are shattered, they only reveal an unfathomable "nowhere," a "liminal space inside which Quinn is suspended, perpetually on the verge of uncovering some great mystery, while remaining interminably on the surface, not so much looking in as looking back at a distorted image of himself and the space he inhabits" (Swope 13). That space is the labyrinthine city/text which mirrors the sublime complexity of the self, especially apprehended in its "meta" condition: "if the self is a text, and if a text's knowability is endlessly deferred, referring within the cognitive process only to other texts (be they physical texts or other selves), then 'true' self-knowledge is impossible" (Kerby qtd. in Alford "Mirrors" n. p.). This is why Quinn has no other choice by the end of the novel than to eventually retreat into Stillman Jr.'s dark room and vanish from the text when there are no more pages left for words to remain and for him to exist.

Reinventing Solitude

What Michel and Quinn also experience in their urban wanderings and transcriptions is the loneliness associated with the task of writing. Their solitude, however, comes from two different practices of the city. On the one hand, Auster's protagonist seems to be a true descendent of the *flâneur*, engulfed by the size and speed of the urban crowd while, on the other hand, Belletto's character is confronted with the solitude of a deserted city during a particularly hot month of August.

Auster's New York is a labyrinth; Belletto's Lyon a static hell. Michel Soler, whose homophonic surname already prophesizes his solar fate (in French Soler is pronounced like *solaire*, i.e. solar), is drifting under the murderous sun in the same way he seems to be at the burning center of everything. Events gravitate around Michel in a grotesque cycle which is both humorous and sinister and described through Belletto's usually hyperbolic style, such as in the following passage:

> The splashing of the fountain in the square reawakened dreams of coolness and lightness. But alas, the heat, the appalling, insalubrious, murderous heat of a city in a continental climate (heat that shattered all records in Lyon that summer), merely seemed the more oppressive, a heat to expire in, 160 degrees in the shade at the very least. Out in the sun, impossible to gauge, there was no one foolhardy enough to venture out and set up a thermometer in direct sunlight, certainly not with any hope of coming back in. The thermometers themselves ran screaming back into the shade. (4)

The heat is accompanied by a "light, so violent and so uniform [it looks] like black night" (142). This idea is reminiscent of Edmund Burke's conception of the sublime when he states that "darkness is more productive of sublime ideas than light […] [but] [e]xtreme light, by overcoming the organs of sight, obliterates all objects, so as in its effect exactly to resemble darkness" (Burke 80). Belletto's novel indeed has clear sublime and grotesque overtones (I won't have space to discuss the grotesque aspect of his novels here although it is a key concept to understand his work and metacognitive mystery tales in general).

Michel lives in a state of sheer loneliness in the abandoned city of Lyon. For Burke, "absolute and entire *solitude*, that is, the total and perpetual exclusion from all society, is as great a positive pain as can almost be conceived" (43). The philosopher adds that "an entire life of solitude contradicts the purposes of our being, since death itself is scarcely an idea of more terror" (43). Like Hawthorne's Wakefield, Melville's Bartleby or Auster's characters, Belletto's detective appears as a death-in-life figure whose loneliness feeds his madness and urges him to act in the most unnatural and unexplainable ways.

Moreover, as in Baudelaire's poem "Anywhere Out of the World,"[3] Michel, like Quinn, seems to develop outside accepted, stable categories of space and time. In *City of Glass* Auster takes the time to quote Baudelaire's decentered poetics and reflects upon the complex interplay between space and selfhood:

> Baudelaire: Il me semble que je serais toujours bien là où je ne suis pas. In other words: It seems to me that I will always be happy in the place where I am not. Or, more bluntly: Wherever I am not is the place where I am myself. Or else, taking the bull by the horns: Anywhere out of the world. (132)

Auster's digression on Baudelaire's "Anywhere Out of the World"—a poem which originally stressed a desire to escape from a life of boredom and despair—follows a lengthy description of life in the city, one which lists a series of characters caught in the throes of various forms of social and psychological isolation. "These beggars and performers […] locked inside madness" (130-1) constitute the crowd in which Auster's *flâneur* seems to be at ease and able to feel "out of the world." Auster's appropriation of Baudelaire also points at a desire to convert spatial and mental disorientation into an art, one described by Jacques Attali in his plea for patience and the pleasure of losing one's way (Attali). Quinn, however, does not succeed in mastering this new practice of the labyrinthine city; he cannot appreciate the artistry and design of the maze he lives in. Rather, he feels that he is trapped in a confining nowhere which, in fact, could be anywhere and thus could as well be the few square meters of a dark locked room where he will eventually disappear.

In the same way, Michel Soler often feels alienated, a stranger to his own life, everywhere and nowhere at the same time:

> Around half-past eleven torpor engulfed me. The two dining room windows opened onto a night so anonymous it might have been in a tropical bay. If I stayed this way till daylight, would the sun rise on a tropical bay? On the infinite sea, on vast expanses of virgin nature, on the first day of the world?

> Yes, we might easily have been somewhere else. […] in
> this landscape on the outskirts of Villeurbanne where
> it seemed to be the outpost or the last stop in a cursed
> land. (14)

This passage interestingly reflects the detective's situation in a state of
endless introspection. The questions that Michel keeps asking himself
cannot find answers. He will remain, like Poe's "Man of the Crowd,"
"absorbed in contemplation" (475): "I returned to the contemplation
of other things, that is to say of nothing and everything" (6).

What is difficult to cope with for these characters is the randomness of the things happening to them. Michel Soler, like the sun above
his head, is the core around which events seem to gravitate and crash
according to the forces of chance, or fate, as he has it: "fate was hast-
ily tossing me whole acres of events, making of me its free prisoner!"
(146). And later: "Everything was moving quickly and fate went on
dealing me events endlessly the way a full-fledged neurotic deals
cards on a big winning night, I scarcely had time to pick up and sort
my hand" (194). The city's emptiness reflects the detective's life, beset
by doubt at the beginning as well as at the end of the novel in a loop
effect characteristic of the metacognitive branch of detective fiction:
"Yes, perhaps life would flee, and tomorrow never come. And this
past month of August, what I had lived through, would fall into the
retribution of oblivion, somewhere, nowhere, like a letter written and
never sent [suicide letter]. Master of all I surveyed, I found myself
alone in my deserted city. I did not know" (310).

Such insecurity is counterbalanced by Michel's perfect knowledge
of Lyon and its suburbs. Names of neighborhoods, streets, rivers, and
bridges are indeed systematically given in the novel, providing a realistic setting that contrasts with the incredible story that is told. Nonetheless, the city and its periphery also contribute to the grotesque
and nightmarish atmosphere of the book. This is, for example, what
Michel describes while driving his red Dauphin on his way to visit his
mother:

> I started up. […] the city was dead, it had given up the
> ghost during the night of July 31 and August 1, I had

to drive all the way to the light on Place Grandclément
before I encountered a living soul, and even then to be
candid not much of a soul and not much living, two old
folks prevented by the severity of their infirmities from
fleeing the summer [...]. Avenue Ampère, short and
ugly, flared up. Chemin du Regard, the horrible Chemin du Regard, running alongside the sinister Jonage
Canal. I drew up in front of the house where I was born,
almost my birthplace, a dingy wood cottage, not maintained, infinitely sad in this season and this light, with
the old Cusset Cemetery nearby, the gloomiest of the
gloomy, and the hydroelectric plant, straight out of a
nightmare. (10-1)

The topography generates uncanny emotions within Michel who, although he knows every corner of the city, feels lost, torn between his
roles of detective, criminal, and victim. He does not know if he is the
actor or the spectator of his quest. His life has been obliterated by the
power of the sun, whose light is equivalent to a great darkness that
leaves him tormented in the shadows of doubt, as Michel himself
concludes: "No way of finding out. A thousand ethereal possibilities
arose. We would never know. In any case he was dead now, ethereal
himself. That was the only reality. [...] There were no certainties, no
avenues in which to channel thought or energy. We were still more
or less at square one. There was nothing to do but wait" (204). The
barren city of Lyon thus appears to be an as uncompromising hell
as Baudelaire's Paris, Hawthorne and Poe's London, or Auster's New
York. It is a space where the metacognitive investigator can only get
lost, not merely on the street, but within himself, forced to face questions that, for better or for worse, will remain unanswered.

NOTES

1. This is already clear in "The Blue Cross" in which Valentin, the French detective,
   is amazed by Father Brown's intuitive method and his final claim to the villain
   Flambeau: "Lord bless you, we have to know twenty such things when we work
   among the criminal classes!" (Chesterton 22).

2. In Belletto's novel, the event becomes a *mise en abyme* when the reader discovers that the whole criminal machinery was set in motion because Isabel de Tuermas, one of the key characters to the mystery, answered the phone taking on the identity of her nearly-twin-sister, acting "out of curiosity" (292). One more intriguing and fascinating link between Belletto's and Auster's texts is that Michel Soler has a dream in which he wanders through the streets of New York just when he is thinking about hiring a private detective to help him solve the mystery in which he is involved (150).

3. "Anywhere Out of the World/N'importe où hors du monde" was published in *Le Spleen de Paris* (1869).

WORKS CITED

Alford, Steven E. "Mirrors of Madness: Paul Auster's *The New York Trilogy*." *Critique: Studies in Contemporary Fiction*, vol. 37, no. 1, Fall 1995, pp. 17-33. ProQuest, doi: 10.1080/00111619.1995.9936478.

——. "Spaced-out: Signification and Space in Paul Auster's *The New York Trilogy*." *Contemporary Literature*, vol. 36, no. 4, Winter 1995, pp. 613-32. EBSCO, doi: 10.2307/1208943.

Attali, Jacques. *The Labyrinth in Culture and Society: Pathways to Wisdom*. 1996. Translated by Joseph Rowe, North Atlantic Books, 1999.

Auster, Paul. *The New York Trilogy*. 1985, 1986, 1986. Penguin Books, 1990.

Belletto, René. *Eclipse*. Translated by Jeremy Leggatt, Mercury House Inc., 1990.

Benjamin, Walter. *Charles Baudelaire: A Lyric Poet in the Era of High Capitalism*. Translated by Harry Zohn, New Left Books, 1973.

Burke, Edmund. *A Philosophical Enquiry into the Origin of Our Ideas of the Sublime and the Beautiful*. 1757. U of Notre Dame P, 1958.

Chesterton, Gilbert Keith. "The Blue Cross." *The Father Brown Stories*. 1910. Cassell and Company, 1948, pp. 9-23.

Dechêne, Antoine. *Detective Fiction and the Problem of Knowledge:*

Perspectives on the Metacognitive Mystery Tale. Palgrave MacMillan, 2018.

Ewert, Jeanne C. "'A Thousand Other Mysteries': Metaphysical Detection, Ontological Quests." *Detecting Texts: The Metaphysical Detective Story from Poe to Postmodernism*, edited by Patricia Merivale and Susan Elizabeth Sweeney, U of Pennsylvania P, 1999, pp. 179-98.

Haycraft, Howard. *Murder for Pleasure: The Life and Times of the Detective Story*. Peter Davies, 1942.

Holquist, Michael. "Whodunit and Other Questions: Metaphysical Detective Stories in Post-war Fiction." *New Literary History*, vol. 3., no. 1, 1971, pp. 135-56. JSTOR, www.jstor.org/stable/468384.

Kugler, Mathias. *Paul Auster's The New York Trilogy as Postmodern Detective Fiction*. Diplomarbeiten Agentur, 1999.

Marcus, Laura. "Detection and Literary Fiction." *The Cambridge Companion to Crime Fiction*, edited by Martin Priestman, Cambridge UP, 2003, pp. 245-67.

Margolies, Edward. *New York and the Literary Imagination: The City in Twentieth Century Fiction and Drama*. McFarland & Company, 2008.

Merivale, Patricia, and Susan Elizabeth Sweeney. "The Game's Afoot: On the Trail of the Metaphysical Detective Story." *Detecting Texts: The Metaphysical Detective Story From Poe to Postmodernism*, edited by Patricia Merivale and Susan Elizabeth Sweeney, U of Pennsylvania P, 1999, pp. 1-24.

Poe, Edgar Allan. "The Man of the Crowd." 1840. *The Complete Tales and Poems of Edgar Allan Poe*. 1840. Vintage Books, 1975, pp. 475-81.

Robbe-Grillet, Alain. *The Erasers*. 1953. Translated by Richard Howard, Grove Press, 1964.

Schmid, David. "From the Locked Room to the Globe: Space in Crime Fiction." *Cross-Cultural Connections in Crime Fiction*, edited by Vivien Miller and Helen Oakley, Palgrave MacMillan, 2012, pp. 7-23.

Shiloh, Ilana. *Paul Auster and Postmodern Quests: On the Road to Nowhere*. Peter Lang, 2002.

Swope, Richard. "Supposing a Space: The Detecting Subject in Paul Auster's *City of Glass*." *Reconstruction: Studies in Contemporary Culture*, 2002, pp. 1-17.

Worthington, Heather. *Key Concepts in Crime Fiction*. Palgrave MacMillan, 2011.

"Where Things Happen": Toxic Masculinity and Mike Hammer's New York City

Alexander N. Howe

"Guys like you can't escape the city. Hell, you a got a blood contract with this place. You're married to the old girl." — Mickey Spillane and Max Collins, *Kiss Her Goodbye* (2011).

Abstract

After the Second World War, American literature opened more broadly to formerly silenced voices through various "booms" in Latin American and ethnic literatures, as well as a profusion of genre fiction authored by women. In crime fiction, there is unsurprisingly a great re-entrenchment of the white male perspective; and in the 1950s, there is no better example than Mickey Spillane's Mike Hammer, the racist, misogynist, hyper-masculine, homicidal private investigator who policed the exceptionally "mean" New York City streets acting as judge, jury, and executioner. Mike Hammer is a great monument to white masculinity as it tries to defend itself against social change, and the series actually runs through the mid-1990s and contains thirteen novels (excluding the Hammer novels later completed by Max Allan Collins). Mickey Spillane famously said that he disliked New York City, but that was "where things happened," and throughout these novels the city plays an active—and certainly gendered—role in narration. The detective's division of the city into good, bad, and damned neighborhoods is based on broad racist and classist assumptions that is mediated—albeit intermittently—by the comparably more nuanced vision of his secretary, collaborator, and (ultimately) fiancée, Velda. On several occasions, Velda completes brief investigative work and reads the city in a remarkably different and inclusive fashion from the more dismissive sleuth, revealing the blind spots of his violently biased viewing. Leslie Kern's work, *Feminist City: Claiming Space in a Man-Made World* (Verso 2020), has deservedly caught the attention of numerous disciplines of the academy and offers an apt platform for examining the ways in which our urban environments are built to discriminate. This article will read Hammer's New York City through this lens.

Introduction

After the Second World War, in American crime fiction there is, unsurprisingly, a great re-entrenchment of the white male perspective, and beginning in the late 1940s, there is no better example of this reaction than Mickey Spillane's Mike Hammer. Spillane's detective is a notoriously racist, misogynist, hyper-masculine, homicidal private investigator who polices the exceptionally "mean" New York City streets acting as judge, jury, and executioner. Mike Hammer is a great monument to white masculinity as it tries to defend itself against social change, and the series actually runs through the mid-1990s and contains thirteen novels, though Max Allan Collins will go on to complete twelve additional works from Spillane's draft manuscripts. Throughout these novels, the city plays an active and certainly gendered role in narration, as the detective divides the city into good, bad, and damned neighborhoods based upon broad racist, classist, and sexist assumptions. This essay analyzes Spillane's authentication of New York City through Hammer's violence (and vice versa) and explores the ways this relationship is mediated—albeit intermittently—by the presence of his secretary, collaborator, and ultimately fiancée, Velda. On several occasions, Velda completes investigative work in a way that disrupts the reliability of Hammer's violently biased narration of the city, and her independence and accomplishments make her remarkable within the history of hard-boiled detective fiction.

The Detective in the City: The Language of Violence

The detective story is of course inextricably bound to the emergence of the nineteenth-century city. Edgar Allan Poe's Paris, Anna Katharine Green's New York City, Wilkie Collins' and Sir Arthur Conan Doyle's London all set the stage for the urban focus of the detective, who emerges to order the chaos of the new metropolis. In this compressed and fast-moving space, former boundaries of class, gender, race, and decorum are—in crucial moments—fluid. The newspaper and magazine culture that flourished at this time capitalized on this tumult by publishing countless stories of urban crime, and as Dana Brand has suggested, the stage was set for an "urban observer," like the detective, who could "read and in some sense master" the illegibility of the city (89). As critics have long indicated, the city is itself a mystery that must be interpreted in parallel with the larger mystery of the detective story (Bershady 73). The classical detective template for this expertise is typified in "The Red-Headed League" (1891), when Sherlock Holmes makes the grand claim: "It is a hobby of mine to have an exact knowledge of London" (Doyle 61). Doyle's detective proves his facility and ease with the city throughout the series through his myriad of disguises, safe havens, and trusted informants. With the benefit of the detective's wisdom, the reader gains the narrative peace of the solution to the crime and, as Harold Bershady suggests, is made "more comfortable and safe to partake of the city with greater sureness, [and] not to feel a hesitant stranger in the city that is a large part of his or her life" (73). The detective makes the city knowable by reducing it to a case that might be solved, even retroactively, and Bershady's reminder that this is as much practical knowledge and know-how as it is a larger epistemological manifesto is important to note. The detective story invites us all to become, in a limited way, urbanists and urban geographers.

Such readings are drawn in large part from the totalizing view of the classical detective like Sherlock Holmes, which stands in sharp contrast to the limited vision of the hard-boiled sleuth. In the case of the latter, the detective lacks immunity from danger, and consequently he cannot muse over the city as an object of knowledge or enmesh himself quite so seamlessly into urban space. Glenn Most summarizes this well when he playfully suggests that we have no idea where Sam Spade, Philip Marlowe, and Lew Archer shop for groceries (70). These characters are likely the greatest literary representatives of San Francisco and Los Angeles; yet regardless of how intimate this connection seems, it remains in large part thinly drawn and atmospheric. Lee Horsley offers some insight into this inherent paradox when he reads hard-boiled crime fiction as "a political myth containing the contradictions and ironies that bedeviled the efforts to adjust liberal ideas to the demands of an industrialized, urbanized nation" (75). The rough contradictions of the hard-boiled dick stand in stark contrast to the genteel synthesis of the classical gentleman sleuth. The hard-boiled detective can be seen as an assemblage of ideas meant to answer the inherent complexities and contradictions of urban life, but the answers he offers are limited to say the least, and the manageable tale suggested by Horsley is always in danger of devolving into a violent masculinity of endurance akin to the Western.

Raymond Chandler's "The Simple Art of Murder" (1944) is as much a response to this inherent danger of generic violence as it is a diatribe aimed at the British tradition of countryside mysteries. This piece is frequently taken as a celebration of the grittiness of the "mean streets" that are the detective's domain—and it is partially this—but more importantly it is a celebration of the inherent literary possibilities of the American hard-boiled school, written with an eye toward his own project and as an homage to Dashiell Hammett, whom Chandler credits for raising detective fiction to the level of an art. There is no need for an extensive repetition of oft-quoted material from this piece, but there are a few items worth recalling. Chandler suggests that "[a]ll language begins with speech, and the speech of common men," which is precisely the milieu of the hard-boiled detective who is "common man" and has a "sense of character" (17). Common American speech is given primary value, and the authenticity of this speech authorizes the literariness of the type of detective fiction that Chandler is trying to affirm. As he writes near the conclusion of the essay, the detective "talks as the man of his age talks—that is, with rude wit, a lively sense of the grotesque, a disgust for sham, and a contempt for pettiness" (20-21). Hammett writes with an immediacy for readers with a "sharp, aggressive attitude to life" and a fearless taste for the "seamy side" of things, which is "right down their street" (16). Presumably, there is an authentic voice in Hammett's writing when it is at its best—although, Chandler does admit that the author devolves into clichéd narrative when he is at his worst.

For Chandler, "mean streets" is in large part a metaphor for a certain type of speech, and the final importance here is the development of character, "which is all the detective story has any right to be about anyway," as he notes (19). The emphasis upon "street" is in part rooted in the *flânerie* of the nineteenth century that influenced Poe's detective narratives and methods (Brand 105); however, the mean streets of the hard-boiled world are distinctly modern and brimming with disarray. In keeping with Chandler's emphasis upon language, and his penchant for jarring metaphors, the very notion of "street" likewise resonates with meaning, but in a particularly hard-boiled fashion. Todd Christianson distinguishes hard-boiled conceit, "colloquial and poignant metaphors and similes" (151), from "tough talk," which is a "linguistic assertion of power over experience" (153) through the threat of violence. The tough talk, wit, and wisecracks of the hard-boiled detective quickly become formulaic, but for Christianson hard-boiled conceit is as sophisticated as the linguistic play in the works of Modernists like T.S. Eliot (158). To these ends, Christianson compares Eliot's complex metaphors and similes (e.g. "spread out against the sky/Like a patient etherized upon a table" from "The Love Song of J. Alfred Prufrock,") with two well-known similes from Chandler: "face like a collapsed lung" and "mouth like wilted lettuce" (qtd. 158-59). Such descriptions "resist literal visualization, but convey a multivalent perception of reality which resists verbalization" (159), Christianson notes. This stylistic play highlights the detective's struggle to make meaning, and in the end his sharp-witted narration and solutions to crimes are "undermined by the chaos and disorder of contemporary experience which the narration has revealed and attempted to control and order" (161). While Chandler's "mean streets" obviously suggests violence, the greater feat for the detective is to remain "neither tarnished nor afraid" (18) in the face of his inevitably doomed narration.

In her reassessment of Chandler's discussion of realism and authenticity in detective fiction, Malcah Effron examines the tendency for contemporary authors to include actual details of the city in their work such that the novels read as virtual street atlases. Edinburgh in Ian Rankin's Rebus series and Oxford in Colin Dexter's Morse novels are prime examples of this practice (331). The logic of this gesture is that real settings and street names encourage the reader to suspend disbelief and accept the story as realistic. In contrast, Chandler's realism was based upon the authentic speech of his characters, and the streets of his Los Angeles receive nowhere near the narrative detail of Sara Paretsky's Chicago, for example. Paretsky's V.I. Warshawski frequently describes actual locations in her city, thus establishing the authority of her story based upon her status as a Chicagoan. Her knowledge of the "physical environment" authorizes her "representation of its social environment" (339). However, as Effron suggests, details of the city are ultimately extraneous to the mystery puzzles of detective narrative—a familiarity with Michigan Avenue may suspend a reader's disbelief, but this reference is never a clue crucial to the solution of the crime. The result is that realism based upon place is as suspect as realism based upon speech. As Effron concludes, "Thus, contemporary detective fiction's topographically accurate settings highlight the failure of speech or texts to present an authentic experience of reality" (345). For both Christianson and Effron, then, the hard-boiled fascination with the gritty reality of the streets is ultimately an expression of the limits of the detective's ability to make sense of the world and provide a sound narrative of authenticity. While authors like Chandler and Paretsky examine this limitation to produce more complex literary expressions, Mickey Spillane follows a quite different path.

Mike Hammer and the Authenticity of Violence

Mickey Spillane's first novel, *I, the Jury* (1947), catapulted the author to literary infamy. His brutish detective is the perfect distillation of the most base and thoughtless hard-boiled elements, and this first novel prompted Anthony Boucher to brand Spillane's writing as "derivative" and suitable for "required reading in a Gestapo training school" (qtd. Davis 7), a sentiment that *Time* magazine echoed later in 1951 when it famously summarized the author's work as "sexy drivel" (qtd. Corliss). Nevertheless, for the next fifty years after the publication of this first work, Spillane produced another twelve Mike Hammer novels, and after his death in 2006, his literary executor, Max Collins, has finished an additional twelve Hammer novels based on Spillane's outlines and drafts. Despite the critical panning exemplified by Boucher, Spillane was a perennial bestseller in his lifetime, and he himself claimed to be the fifth most translated author in the world— purportedly losing out to only Lenin, Tolstoy, Gorky, and Verne (Davis 7). Historically, this is near the end of the productive period of the original hard-boiled authors, but Lewis Moore still considers Spillane a part of the "early period" of hard-boiled fiction, and he goes so far as to group the author with the likes of Daly, Hammett, Chandler, and Macdonald as "set[ting] the early boundaries of the genre" (4). Chandler's Marlowe and Spillane's Hammer, in Moore's reading, mark the "beginning fragmentation of the heroic image of the hard-boiled detective," an understatement in the case of Spillane, to be sure (35). The self-conscious and often skeptical knightly code of Marlowe is nowhere to be found in Hammer, who incessantly revels in the sort of unseemly violence that prior detectives experienced with great trepidation and only when provoked beyond their breaking point.

Without question, Mike Hammer represents the literary zenith of what is now referred to as toxic masculinity. In the first Hammer novel, *I, the Jury*, the violence of this guise and relationship to speech is summarized early in the novel after the murder of Mike Hammer's war buddy, Jack Williams. As the detective vows vengeance to his police lieutenant friend (and foil) Pat Chambers, "A jury is cold and impartial like they're supposed to be, while some snotty lawyer makes them pour tears as he tells how his client was insane at the moment or had to shoot in self-defense. Swell. The law is fine. But this time I'm the law and I'm not going to be cold and impartial. I'm going to remember all those things" (*I, the Jury* 7). The rhetoric of this famous line is heightened with Hammer's grisly dramatization of the death of Jack, who suffered an amputation during the war, and was shot in the stomach while the killer watched him drag himself across the floor before finishing the job. When Hammer says he is going to "remember all those things," he is at the same time revealing the authenticity of his own language, which is of course the language of violence. The existence of evil in the world (here theatrically done to a comrade in arms) underwrites Hammer's violence. The authenticity of this brazenness is repeated throughout the entire series—often in such scenarios of revenge—and is figured in both Hammer's beastly stature and deeds. Indeed, such comments are a part of Spillane's template, and each Hammer novel begins with the detective reminding Pat Chambers, or anyone who will listen, that the world is a violent place and this violence must be met in kind.

This raw, vengeful brutality of Mike Hammer is inextricably linked to New York City in the series. As Spillane said in an interview with *Crime Time Magazine* shortly before his death in 2006, "I hate New York. But that's where things happen, so I use it as a base for stories, I know enough about it. But I have to keep going back there" (Carlson). Elsewhere in this same interview, the author discusses his annual research trips to the city and the mass of changes that he had witnessed throughout the years: "'The face of the city changes. The city's almost alive, you can see the movement of people from one section to another'" (Carlson). This sense of movement through time and space is a part of each Hammer novel, and Max Collins summarizes this well in his finished version of Spillane's draft manuscript, *Kiss Her Goodbye*: "'Guys like you can't escape the city. Hell, you a got a blood contract with this place. You're married to the old girl'" (Spillane and Collins). The novel takes place in Florida where Hammer recuperates after a mafia shoot out, but the detective is as bound to New York City as Philip Marlowe is to Los Angeles, and his departure does not last for long.

New York City obviously has a long history of American literary fascination, and for the initiated it is difficult even to conceive of the present city without the echoes of versions drafted by Edgar Allan Poe, Herman Melville, Henry James, and Edith Wharton. Christoph Lindner has described this condensation of past and present in the city: "[B]oth the hovering other-worldliness of the skyline and the mobile, performative practices of the sidewalk belong to a broad set of interrelating spatial and cultural dynamics that, together, generated modern New York as both a place and an idea, and that continue even now to shape this endlessly mutable city" (198). This simultaneously ground-level and stratospheric experience, produced by the sublime splendor of the skyline and canyons of avenues and alleyways alike, results in a "street culture dominated by speed, movement, and dislocation" (Lindner 198). Indeed, New York City is all too often the defining example of urban life. There is a straightforwardness in its dissonance that distinguishes it from cities like Los Angeles or even a smaller site like Washington, D.C. The city as a dual text of surface decorum tenuously balanced on a foundation of crime is a leitmotif in all detective stories placed in Los Angeles, and the "Hollywood novel" is itself a genre that highlights the grim realities lurking below the thin veneer of Hollywood theatrics. Similarly, Lucy Andrew and Catherine Phelps speak of the duality of any detective novel featuring a capital city, as these stories "illuminate the connections between the shady and respectable faces of the city and, consequently, point to the disturbing duality of urban space," a discord that the detective must then mediate through the solution to the crime of the story (2-3). Such an unmasking in the case of New York City is entirely superfluous, as privilege and criminality exist in far greater proximity—at least as an idea and experience, if not in neighborhoods and residential addresses. New York City, then, becomes an ideal space for the authenticity of hard-boiled tough talk and endurance that are essential to the hard-boiled ethos.

New York City itself serves not simply as the space of Hammer's violence, but as its guarantor or alibi. In Spillane's second novel, *My Gun is Quick* (1950), the story, interestingly, opens in a second person address with a meta-reflection upon the reading process. Hammer speaks of sitting in front of a warm fire at home and asks if we ever think about what happens outside that space: "Probably not. You pick up a book and read about things and stuff, getting a vicarious kick from people and events that never happened. You're doing it now, getting ready to fill in a normal life with the details of someone else's experiences. Fun isn't it? You read about life on the outside thinking of how maybe you'd like it to happen to you, or at least how you'd like to watch it" (*My Gun* 153). This direct address to the reader on the process and pleasures of reading is remarkable, particularly in hard-boiled fiction. In many ways this reads as Spillane's version of Chandler's "The Simple Art of Murder," as it addresses the inherent escapism of the mystery genre and the comforting pleasures of its uncertainty and intrigue. However, remaining true to his style, Spillane turns the conversation to a grittier reality that denies such distracting entertainment. To these ends, he compares New York City to the Roman Coliseum: "There isn't a Coliseum any more, but the city is a bigger bowl, and it seats more people. The razor-sharp claws aren't those of wild animals but man's can be just as sharp and twice as vicious. You have to be quick, and you have to be able, or you become one of the devoured, and if you can kill first, no matter how and no matter who, you can live and return to the comfortable chair by the fire" (*My Gun* 153). Naturally, it is Mike Hammer who remains quick enough to survive the competition that is suggested in this passage and the title of the novel. As was already established in *I, the Jury*, the detective can equal any criminal's violence. Not only is this his preference, but it is also what is required by the city itself. This passage is especially telling given Mike Hammer's incessant claims to a ferocious—and therefore authentic—manhood, based upon the guise of plain-speaking recognition and knowledge of the city's violence. However, the chosen vehicle of expression here is a melodramatic metaphor deserving of Hollywood. Though many of his expressions of this imperative to violence are less overwrought, the strained generic conventions that make up such claims to authenticity reveal themselves at every turn.

The figure of the Coliseum is a hyperbolic description that borders on camp; however, it is not so far from hard-boiled masculinity counterpoised against the city that is suggested, for example, in

Dashiell Hammett's *Red Harvest* (1929) or Raymond Chandler's *Farewell, My Lovely* (1940). Hammett's work offers a bloody, Hobbesian vision of the vicious Personville, which is aptly referred to as Poisonville by the locals, just as Chandler's text follows the violent wake of Moose Malloy, and his even more dangerous beloved little Velma, through the streets of Los Angeles. Hammett's piece takes place in a small mining town, but it is a clear stand-in for the urban milieu that is about to become the standard for the genre; and while Chandler's work is inevitably a commentary on such versions of masculinity, the pairing of urban spaces with hyper-masculine figures pitted against the environment is basic to the genre. The hero's greatest charge in any narrative is to survive above all else. Mike Hammer's brutality in stature and action is likewise a stock feature of Spillane's novels, and examples of straightforward exposition of these traits abound in the series. In *One Lonely Night* (1951), for example, he avers, "I was a ruthless bastard with a twisted mind who could look on death and find it pleasant. I could break an arm or smash in a face because it was easier that way than asking questions" (144). As is true of so many of these self-descriptions, Hammer admits the extra-moral nature of his disposition and thus endeavors, presumably, to reassure the reader of this honesty. Further, this violent streak is not simple animalistic hostility. He remains a detective, after all, with a modicum of reason and street-savvy wisdom. An apt summation of this reasoned enmity can be found in *The Big Kill* (1951): "I don't like people. I don't like any kind of people. When you get them together in a big lump they all get nasty and dirty and full of trouble. So I don't like people including you. That's what a misanthropist is" (178). Mike Hammer is murderous and often indistinguishable from the criminals he hunts; however, he does know what a misanthrope is and admits to this temperament.

A Cemetery of the Buildings: Mike Hammer's New York City

The Hammer novels include a smattering of real sites in New York City, and Spillane prefers to contextualize his work with broader set pieces of neighborhoods and streets and avenues. As an example of the former, *One Lonely Night* begins memorably on the George Washington Bridge (5); *My Gun is Quick* finds Hammer "under the el on Third Avenue" (165); the New York City Library appears in *The Snake* (1964) (450); and in *The Girl Hunters* (1962), Hammer looks reflectively at the Paramount Building and later the New York Tribune Building (41; 98). Neighborhoods and vague street addresses are mentioned quite frequently, and typically fall into a dichotomy of the tony and the damned. In *I, the Jury*, the psychoanalyst, Charlotte Manning, keeps an office on Park Avenue catering to "ritzy clientele" (13); *Vengeance is Mine!* (1950) explores the motley spaces in Times Square and the Bowery (385); *My Gun is Quick* features the Long Island mansion of the industrialist Berins-Grotin, as well as a "fancy residential section" of Brooklyn and a description of the bustling Village by night (174; 260; 261); and the Flatbush neighborhood in Brooklyn is a repeated location in *The Girl Hunters* (267; 291).

Streets and avenues feature frequently in the Hammer novels, lending value and judgment as metaphors and metonyms within the narration, but also acting as corridors through the city that offer the detective time for reflection. Hammer's workaday disgust for Wall Street, Park Avenue, and Central Park South are obvious examples, which appear frequently. A more nuanced example is a description of slums on the East Side in *The Big Kill*. As Hammer trails a suspect, he remarks, "It was one of those shabby blocks a few years from condemnation. The sidewalks were littered with ancient baby buggies, a horde of kids playing in the garbage on the sidewalks and people on the stoops who didn't give a damn what the kids did so long as they could yap and slop beer" (196). Hammer's defense of the working class has little patience for the working poor, and this economic judgment becomes racialized at other moments in the series. As charming sensory background for *The Girl Hunters*, Hammer poetically describes "supper smells in ten languages" that waft in as he opens a window in an apartment near Times Square (41). However, in *One Lonely Night* (1950), he drives to the edge of Harlem, a place he describes as a "strange no-man's-land where the white mixed with the black and languages overflowed into each other like that of the horde around the Tower of Babel. There were strange, foreign smells of cooking and too many people in too few rooms. There were hostile eyes of children who became suddenly silent as you passed" (133). Clearly, New York's changing demographics, and the growing African American and Puerto Rican populations in Harlem, make the typically unflappable detective uncomfortable. Brian Tochterman summarizes this well when he identifies this confluence of slum life and crime as Spillane's primary "examples of forces tearing apart the comfortable white working-class city that xenophobes like Hammer cherished" (50-51). This aversion is captured in moments like the beginning of *One Lonely Night* when Hammer imagines that he might run away and take Velda to a "small community where murder and guns and dames didn't happen" (9). Though he frequently identifies himself with the rough chaos of the city, in this moment, the detective contemplates white flight to the suburbs.

Spillane consistently includes streets as markers of value and authenticity that support the harsh—and stylized—realism of the city that Spillane self-consciously depicts. As Hammer asserts in *Kiss Me, Deadly* (1952), "This is New York. Something exciting is happening every minute. After a while you get used to it and don't pay much attention to it" (433). Hammer and his police captain friend Pat Chambers speak of neighborhoods where murder isn't "uncommon" and a killing is "neither important nor interesting enough to drag out the local citizenry in a downpour" (*One Lonely* 114; *Big Kill* 181). New York is indeed "where things happen," and this sort of violence is read as part of the life force of the city itself. The detective memorably personifies this in *Kiss Me, Deadly*, as he muses, "The voice of the monster [i.e., the city] outside the glass was a constant drone, but when you listened long enough it became a flat, sarcastic sneer that pushed ten million people into bigger and better troubles, and then the sneer was heard for what it was, a derisive laugh that thought blood running from an open wound was funny, and death was the biggest joke of all" (381). The city and its streets described as a monster is a common figure in the series. For example, in *One Lonely Night*, Hammer reports that "[t]he street boasted a lone light a hundred yards away, a wan, yellow eye that seemed to search for us with eerie tendrils, determined to pull us into the glare" (49). This hardness of the city is given a variety of images. For example, Hammer describes it as a "a steel forest that climbed into the sky," but this is softened, sarcastically, when he speaks of elevators in posh apartment buildings that "went up to heaven" (*One Lonely* 130; *Big Kill* 202). Elsewhere, he speaks of the rain turning Manhattan into a city of reflections, "a city you saw twice no matter where you looked" (*One Lonely* 28), and although this is a labored metaphor, it emphasizes the contradictions that compose Hammer's presentation of New York—and thus himself.

A final word should be said of Hammer's "mean streets" regarding his use of the larger avenues, moving between the uptown to downtown neighborhoods. In these moments, the city is reduced to corridors of meaning and sectors representing broad ideas of poverty, affluence, class, and race. As such, the city represents danger but also moments of pause for reflection. On a drive going south down Ninth Avenue, Hammer talks of "trying to line things up in order. Hell there was no order" (*My Gun* 233). Similarly, as Hammer hops in a cab from downtown to his office, he mentions thinking of the case (the apparent suicide of his friend Chester Wheeler) "all the way uptown" (*Vengeance* 357). In *The Girl Hunters*, after a long walk across town, the detective details the process of picking up a rental car on 49th Street and working his way slowly out of the city on the West Side Drive and on to the New York Thruway to New Paltz while tailing a suspect (102). Such detailed descriptions, and accompanying reflections, are common to the series, and Hammer is certainly always in motion. These moments of transit effectively pause the action of the narrative because the city is so large that it requires considerable time to move from one place to the next.

The melodrama within Spillane's storytelling is interesting in light of Effron's argument regarding the anti-fetishization of speech that occurs with the inclusion of real pieces of urban geography in detective fiction. This is undoubtedly true in the examples that she examines, and it is likely true in moments when reading Spillane. A mention of SoHo, for example, requires a reader's contextualization and associations, thus bolstering authenticity and momentarily disrupting the rhetoric of narration. However, with a force and persistence like no other hard-boiled author, Spillane simultaneously reduces the city and its mean streets to literary props of monstrosity, emergency, nostalgia, and occasional wonder. Indeed, New York City is the primary literary prop with which Spillane draws the savage figure of Mike Hammer himself.

Conclusion: Velda's New York City

Spillane's literary appropriation of the city for his brand of toxic masculinity resonates strongly with the ongoing attention to feminist geography in contemporary criticism. Indeed, as Mike Hammer dons the city as he would a piece of ruggedly fitting clothing, one is reminded of the feminist geographer Jane Darke's famous claim, "Our cities are patriarchy written in stone, brick, glass and concrete" (88). The exceptionally powerful rhetoric of our lived spaces cannot be overstated, although it all too frequently goes unnoticed. Leslie Kern's recent work, *Feminist City: Claiming Space in a Man-made World*, addresses this foundational misogyny built into the architecture and design—and importantly, access to supports and services—in contemporary cities. In her historical account of the rise of the city in the nineteenth century, Kern discusses many of the urban trials that are associated with the rise of detective fiction. Crowded streets allow freedom of movement, at least partially, and distinctions of class and gender (and later race) are made less distinct in many ways. The industrialization that accompanies the new metropolis provides great employment opportunities for lower class men and women, which in turn requires that gender norms change significantly. This change required the emergence of policing and the surveillance apparatuses well known in detective fiction and its criticism. By way of conclusion, I want to review Kern's comments on gentrification and reflect upon the place of Velda, Hammer's dauntless secretary, in the Mike Hammer series.

As Kern emphasizes, the need for segregating safe spaces for well-to-do white women drove a considerable amount of urban development. Here, the author cites the nineteenth century New York Ladies' Mile, a long stretch of exclusive and safe shopping and museum opportunities for upper-class women (100). For the elite classes, such partitioning was necessary to ensure that no well-heeled woman was confused with a "public woman." Women living in poverty, or women working in the sex trade, needed to be regulated and kept in place for cities to thrive—for the right residents. This logic of economic and gendered segregation obviously inheres to this day, especially as gentrification reduces so many urban neighborhoods to airport-like uniformity that promises safe access to upper-middle class consumption. Kern's research included analysis of urban condominiums and mixed-use developments, and she found that advertisements geared especially to women focused on experiences of consumption and leisure, much like the Ladies' Mile of the nineteenth century (102-103). Citing the work of Liz Bondi and Mona Domosh, Kern notes that this ostensible opening of urban spaces to women residents does little more than "create environments in which middle-class feminine identities are fostered and protected" (102). The freedom of women within cities thus remains significantly gendered, and the price of admission continues to shut out a substantial portion of the population.

On the matter of gentrification, Kern recalls Samuel R. Delany's lamentation at the Disney-fication of Times Square, which ended access to experience outside middle-class propriety, like porn theaters and street grifters (169-170). Kern cites a passage from filmmaker Brett Story's response to Delany's piece, claiming that this "'contact at the margins' in cities is a form of transgression against forces of capitalism that police contact across difference. This contact might be transformative of social relations in the city" (170). Such transformative contacts are less likely in the era of gentrification, as "over-surveillance and over-policing hold sway, [and] ordinary sorts of contact are increasingly unlikely and fraught with anxiety" (170). Kern's final suggestions for combatting the consequences of this ongoing segregation include attentiveness to past and present feminist visions for the city and a more rigorous "intersectional analysis" at all levels of urban experience that include BIPOC voices that are rarely brought to the urban planning table (173).

This detour through Kern is helpful, as it highlights one of the primary conflicts embodied in the hard-boiled detective, as described by Horsley. He is a hypermasculine figure, but a considerable portion of his rage is directed to preserve the stasis of his white, middle-class values. Though Mike Hammer effectively identifies himself with New York City, it is of course a literary convention—already established long before Spillane put pen to paper—that he is invoking. Indeed, in the moments when Hammer confronts something like difference within the city, this is either disavowed or ignored by hopping in the next cab headed downtown. In a significant way, then, the Hammer novels promise to cleanse the city, providing just enough local idiosyncrasies to authenticate the product. Though Hammer ultimately identifies his New York City with the white working class, this vision is not so distant from today's mixed use low rises for young urban professionals, surrounded as they are by fast casual restaurants and modish bars meant to embody sleek, clean, and sanitized modern urban living.

Hammer's secretary, Velda, is a remarkable character in hard-boiled fiction, and her uniqueness deserves comment, particularly in light of the inherent misogyny of Hammer's presentation of the city. In *Vengeance is Mine!*, Hammer has his investigator's license suspended, but Velda comes to the rescue, as she has her own PI license—and carries a gun. Hammer gives her the business during his suspension and allows her to investigate the case as she sees fit (358). Similar to Sam Spade's Effie Perine, she is confident and comfortable working in support of the masculine space of the detective office; however, unlike Spade's counterpart, Velda is far more independent and sexualized. Hammer suggests that Velda "would have made a beautiful calendar," but he also praises her acumen, asserting that she "had more on the ball than any of the devil's helpers I had ever seen and could hold me over the barrel without saying a word" (359). She and Hammer are two of kind. She is both "big," "lovely" (359), and as lusty as the detective, and she never shies from his flirtations or inappropriate sexual remarks. While she has free rein in this case, her investigative work takes place in Columbus, Ohio, where she researches the background of Chester Wheeler. While this work is unremarkable—she discovers nothing more than the fact that Chester Wheeler was happily married—she is here an active operative. Back in the city, she does flirt with the criminal boss Clyde Williams, gaining information on his operations, and later in the novel she nearly is raped before Hammer comes to the rescue. Her daring undercover work is not without peril. Near the conclusion of the novel, Velda kills one of Williams's thugs and rushes to the aid of a wounded Hammer (502). She had hidden her gun in a shoulder holster, a decidedly unfeminine choice, which Hammer comments on: "You'll do as a partner. Who'd ever think a girl would be wearing a shoulder rig" (502).

The sexual tension between Hammer and Velda is played upon throughout the novels. In *One Lonely Night*, the two kiss and become engaged for a time. Interestingly, in this novel, Velda again departs the city, this time to research the medical records of the blackmailer, Oscar Deamer, in Nebraska. In *The Big Kill*, Velda works a minor case involving a jewel thief who has fled to Miami, and her relationship with Hammer figures less prominently (190). In fact, Hammer sends Velda to Cuba to tail the jewel thief further, but this is in large part to keep her at a distance, so he can continue his relationship with Marsha Lee. He feels guilty about this, and Velda knows he is up to something—"Women always know" (266)—but she conveniently disappears to work her own investigation for the remainder of the novel. In *Kiss Me Deadly* she plays a supporting role in a mafia investigation by flirting with and collecting information from gangsters and congressmen alike. Later in *The Girl Hunters*, after a long absence, we learn that Velda disappeared seven years earlier while on a case. Hammer shares the discovery that during the war Velda had worked for O.S.S., O.S.I., and an even more "highly secretive group" working in counter-intelligence (134). Hammer is delighted to discover that she is alive, even if she is being hunted by Gorlin, a Soviet agent and ex-Nazi killer. In the next novel, *The Snake*, Hammer speaks of Velda's working during these years "behind the Iron Curtain in the biggest chase scene civilization had ever seen" (214). In a curious moment of tame narration, Hammer speaks of Velda's "peculiar past" that grants her a "strange new subtlety," and he describes her participation in covert acts "across the face of the globe" that resulted in "unaccountable numbers" of deaths throughout European and South American capitals (190; 214). When he final reconnects with Velda in this novel, she is protecting a woman, Sue Devon, and working on her own case; however, the two do reunite and consummate their relationship at last in the conclusion to the novel. In the remaining novels authored by Spillane alone, Velda again completes supporting work for her boss, while occasionally falling into danger and needing rescue. In the final novel, *The Black Alley* (1996), Mike Hammer again proposes to Velda—this time without tentativeness.

Velda is a fascinating and compellingly active female character within the history of hard-boiled fiction, but her triumphs and distinctiveness literally cannot take place in Mike Hammer's New York City. It is not a coincidence that all of Velda's detective work is done out of the city. Indeed, even her time as a Cold War hero defending the West took place far from Manhattan and her boss. In Hammer's New York, which is a violent, confrontational, misogynist space, Velda is reduced to a sexualized tool to capitalize on the lust of men. Though Hammer frequently imagined marriage with his more-than-able assistant, this could never occur in the cruel city that amplified his baser instincts, including his lasciviousness, but also offered an unending series of adversaries to be bested before the damsel could be "possessed." She is a "nice partner to have in the firm," but the "someday…" (*Big Kill* 190) that Hammer frequently promises, cannot occur within Spillane's larger narrative. This prohibition is true for Velda as an active partner maneuvering the city as Hammer does and as an active partner in a committed relationship, be this marriage or otherwise. Both Spillane and Hammer seem interested, at times, in seeing Velda in all her complexity; however, the bulk of her nuance occurs out of the narrative view, and her union with the detective is reduced to a tension of waiting until the conclusion of Spillane's portion of the series. This limit is common to the hard-boiled genre. The detective desires a woman who is his equal physically, intellectually, and sexually, and though he may find her in passing, she cannot share his space within the narrative. Chandler's Ann Riordan and Linda Loring are similar examples of this limit, as is Susan Silverman in Robert Parker's Spenser series. Interestingly in Spillane, this prohibition is figured time and time again through New York City itself.

In Raymond Chandler's *Farewell, My Lovely*, Philip Marlowe meets Moose Malloy, the "big man" who is literally out of scale with the urban environment around him; however, it is this very stature that makes him the ideal citizen of this space, at least from the perspective of the detective's search for an idealized (or "big") man to authorize his quest and protect him from criminals and women alike. Chandler's novel, and his reading of masculinity more broadly, is interesting because, already in 1940, he dismisses the violently gendered foundations upon which the genre is built. Mike Hammer is in many ways Moose Malloy written as detective, minus the insightful incongruence between character and setting that is found in Chandler's work. For Spillane, Hammer is the ideal companion and champion of New York City. He endures and vengefully defends those who cannot protect themselves, yet in the end this amounts to nothing more than a defense of the toxic masculinity that was previously a dangerous limit of the hard-boiled detective's might and reason. In her telling absences, Velda offers a compelling alternative vision and a differently imagined city by bringing into question Hammer's rhetoric of authenticity. Her accomplishments and talents are truly extraordinary in the history of hard-boiled fiction, but sadly Spillane could not devise a way to frame these in Hammer's New York, and in the end, Velda remains only an intermittent dissonance within detective's narrative of violent masculinity.

WORKS CITED

Andrew, Lucy and Catherine Phelps. *Crime Fiction in the City: Capital Crimes*. Wales UP, 2013.

Bershady, Harold J. "Detectives Stories and City Life." *Society*, vol. 44, no. 5, 2007, pp. 70-76. *Academic Search Premier*, doi: 10.1007/s12115-007-9015-y

Brand, Dana. *The Spectator and the City in Nineteenth-Century American Literature*. Cambridge UP, 1991.

Carlson, Michael. Interview with Mickey Spillane. *Crime Time*, 29 June 2002. crimetime.co.uk/interviewing-mickey-spillane/. Accessed 2 February 2021.

Chandler, Raymond. "The Simple Art of Murder" [1944]. *The Simple Art of Murder*, Ballantine, 1950, pp. 1-22.

Christianson, Scott. "Tough Talk and Wisecracks: Language as Power in American Detective Fiction." *Journal of Popular Culture*, vol. 23, no. 2, 1989, pp. 151-162.

Corliss, Richard. "The Prince of Pulp." *Time* 22 July 2006. content. time.com/time/arts/article/0,8599,1217987-1,00.html. Accessed 7 February 2021.

Darke, Jane. "The Man-Shaped City." *Changing Places: Women's Lives in the City*, edited by Chris Booth, et al., Sage, 1996, pp. 2-13.

Davis, J. Madison. "His 'Customers' Were the Jury: Mickey Spillane (1918-2006)." *World Literature Today*, vol. 81, no. 2, March – April 2007, pp. 6-8.

Doyle, Arthur Conan. "The Red-Headed League." *The New Annotated Sherlock Holmes: Volume 1*, edited by Leslie Klinger, W.W. Norton, pp. 41-73.

Effron, Malcah. "Fictional Murders in Real 'Mean Streets': Detective Narratives and Authentic Urban Geographies." *JNT: Journal of Narrative Theory*, vol. 39, no. 3, Fall 2009, pp. 330-346. JSTOR, jstor.org/stable/41427212.

Horsley, Lee. *Twentieth-Century Crime Fiction*. Oxford UP, 2005.

Kern, Leslie. *Feminist City: Claiming Space in a Man-made World*. Verso, 2020.

Lindner, Christoph. *Imagining New York City: Literature, Urbanism, and the Visual Arts, 1890-1940*. Oxford UP, 2015.

Moore, Lewis D. *Cracking the Hard-Boiled Detective: A Critical History from the 1920s to the Present*. McFarland, 2006.

Most, Glenn. "Urban Blues: Detective Fiction and the Metropolitan Sublime." *Yale Review*, vol. 94, no. 1, January 2006, pp. 56-72. *Wiley Online*, doi: 10.1111/j.1467-9736.2006.00056.x.

Sanchez-Arce, Ana. "'Authenticism,' or the Authority of Authenticity." *Mosaic*, vol. 40, no. 3, 2007, pp. 139-55. *JSTOR*, doi: jstor.org/stable/44030269.

Tochterman, Brian L. *The Dying City: Postwar New York and the Ideology of Fear*. U of North Carolina P, 2017.

Spillane, Mickey. *The Big Kill* [1951b]. *The Mike Hammer Collection: Volume 2*. New American Library, 2001, pp. 175-346.

——. *The Black Alley* [1996]. *The Mike Hammer Collection: Volume 4*. New American Library, 2018, pp. 1-173.

——. *The Girl Hunters* [1962]. *The Mike Hammer Collection: Volume 3*. New American Library, 2010, pp. 1-172.

——. *I, the Jury* [1947]. *The Mike Hammer Collection: Volume 1*. New American Library, 2001, pp. 1-148.

——. *Kiss Me, Deadly* [1952]. *The Mike Hammer Collection: Volume 2*. New American Library, 2001, pp. 347-511.

——. *My Gun Is Quick* [1950a]. *The Mike Hammer Collection: Volume 1*. New American Library, 2001, pp. 149-344.

——. *One Lonely Night* [1951a]. *The Mike Hammer Collection: Volume 2*. New American Library, 2001, pp. 1-174.

——. *The Snake* [1964]. *The Mike Hammer Collection: Volume 3*. New American Library, 2010, pp. 173-336.

——. *The Twisted Thing* [1966]. *The Mike Hammer Collection: Volume 3*. New American Library, 2010, pp. 337-507.

——. *Vengeance is Mine!* [1950b]. *The Mike Hammer Collection: Volume 1*. New American Library, 2001, pp. 345-513.

Spillane, Mickey and Max Collins. *Kiss Her Goodbye* [2011]. Titan Books, 2021.

Harlem as the Confluence of Oriental Occultism and Western Rationalism in Rudolph Fisher's *The Conjure Man Dies: A Mystery Tale of Dark Harlem*

Joydeep Bhattacharyya

Abstract

This paper examines how the geospatial reality of Harlem, New York, manifests itself in one of the earliest detective fictions of the twentieth century, the second novel of Rudolph Fisher, *The Conjure Man Dies* (1932). The paper is divided into three sections, with the first section, "Harlem as geopolitical space," surveying how Harlem acts as the general setting of the text, and how this setting affects the narrative thrust of the text. The second section, titled "Harlem as the racial space," expounds upon Harlem as space both defined and limited by the racial and ethnic identities of the African American community. The final section, "Harlem as the melting pot of the Orient and the Occident," investigates how Harlem acts as a space of confluence of knowledge systems surpassing racial identities: that of Oriental occultism, as manifested through the psychist-cum-conjurer Frimbo, and Western rationalism, as manifested through Dr. John Archer and the investigating officers.

Published in 1932, *The Conjure Man Dies: A Mystery Tale of Dark Harlem* is one of the earliest detective fictions about the African American community, written by one of the most vital African American authors, Rudolph Fisher, and published in non-serialized form. The novel is set in the geopolitical space of Harlem, a neighborhood within New York City. The narrative thrust of the novel deals with the assumed and the supposed murder of Frimbo, a conjure man from the African sub-continent, who is quite popular among the locals as a seer, and the ensuing investigation by the team essentially comprising Black members of the police department; Dr. Archer, a Black physician trained in the Western sciences; one of the initial suspects Bubber Brown, who is also Black; and lastly the African conjure man Frimbo himself.

Situating Fisher's *The Conjure Man Dies* within the Genre of Detective Fiction

Firstly, it is imperative to examine Fisher's masterpiece within the theoretical underpinnings of the detective fiction genre. Some eminent Western theorists like P.D James, Tzvetan Todorov, Martin Priestman and others have promulgated the chief characteristics of detective novels. Importantly, Martin Priestman, in *Crime Fiction: From Poe to the Present*, argues that the detective "whodunnit" separates itself from that body of literature that has always been present and has incorporated some kind of crime. Priestman tries to define the term "whodunnit" as a narrative that tries to unravel past events, and in doing so unravels a crime which had been committed, and interestingly, most of the present activity focuses on the detecting activity itself, both by the police as well as the amateur, and the present is rendered static. He further observes, "the detective whodunnit focuses primarily on identifying the perpetrator of a crime which for most of the story or novel already lies in the past" (5). Furthermore, in his cornerstone essay, the "Typology of Detective Fiction," Tzvetan Todorov notes that in detective stories two murders are committed. The first one is committed by the murderer, which acts as the platform for the second story, in which the murderer of the first story is punished by another murderer, the detective himself, whom Todorov believes to be pure and unpunishable, what he calls "detective's immunity" (44-45). Additionally, P.D. James, in *Talking About Detective Fiction*, notes about detective stories,

> What we can expect is a central mysterious crime, usually murder, a closed circle of suspects, each with motive, means, and opportunity for the crime; a detective, either amateur or professional, who comes in like an avenging deity to solve it; and, by the end of the book, a solution which the reader should be able to arrive at by logical deduction from clues inserted in the novel with deceptive cunning, but essential fairness. (5)

In the light of the aforementioned genre, it seems like Rudolph Fisher's *The Conjure Man Dies* does qualify as a classic detective fiction. His novel encompasses almost all the desirable qualities of the genre. The novel has elements reminiscent of the adventure story, gothic story, and domestic fiction. The novel qualifies to be termed a "whodunnit," with the constant focus on the unravelling of the past crime. Moreover, even James' identified characteristics are supported by the novel. But assessing the novel according to Todorov's postulations becomes an arduous affair due to the usage of multiple detectives. Since the protagonist Frimbo also becomes one of the many detectives investigating his own attempted murder, later dubbed as "'felonious assault'" (178), he is killed in the end, and therefore, Frimbo cannot boast of the "detective's immunity," though the other principal detectives, Perry Dart, Dr. John Archer, and Bubber Brown live on to tell the tale.

Significance of *The Conjure Man Dies*

Almost ninety years have passed since Fisher's *The Conjure Man Dies* was published for the first time. Moreover, if not the first of its kind, it definitely is one of the earliest detective fictions written by a member of the African American community. The vibrancy and vitality of such a novel, located in one of the most fertile historical epochs, the Harlem Renaissance, have been pointed out by several scholars. For instance, Lois Brown notes that *The Conjure Man Dies* is "the first non-serialized detective novel by an African American to feature a black sleuth" (166). Reiterating a similar consciousness, Soitos writes, "*The Conjure Man Dies* is the first detective novel to assert proudly its detective themes in a completely black environment with an all-black cast of characters" (93). Elsewhere, it has been noted that though Rudolph Fisher's *The Conjure Man Dies: A Mystery Tale of Dark Harlem* (1932) was not the first detective novel to be penned by a black author, "it was the first 'black identified' detective novel, focused entirely on African American characters and set in Harlem during the Depression era" (Wintz and Finkelman 247). Also, the importance of such a text has been highlighted by Paula Woods, who notes that *The Conjure Man Dies* is landmark fiction, wherein Black characters and themes have been extensively dealt with and put within the dramatic action, "where heretofore they had been only minor characters in novels by whites" (20).

The *Conjure Man Dies* (1932) is a milestone in the genre of African American detective fiction; many genealogical studies mention Fisher's *The Conjure Man*, along with his first novel, *The Walls of Jericho* (1928). Though time and again, passing references have been provided for the setting of the novel, no existing research focuses in its entirety on the city of New York vis-à-vis Harlem, which is the ultimate aim of this paper. Only Mary Condé in her essay, "The 'almost bitter murmur' in Rudolph Fisher's *The Conjure Man Dies*," devotes a small section to the setting of the novel. She notes that, "Fisher himself proposed that Harlem and its black inhabitants were peculiarly appropriate for a detective story" (14), and she notes that in a radio interview which aired in January 1933, Fisher had said,

> Darkness and mystery go together, don't they? The children of the night –and I say this in all seriousness—are children of mystery. The very setting is mystery—outsiders know nothing of Harlem life as it really is...what goes on behind the scenes and beneath the dark skins of Harlem folk—fiction has not found much of that yet. And much of it is perfectly in tune with the best

of mystery tradition—variety, color, mysticism, superstition, malice, and violence. (as qtd. in Conde 14)

Otherwise, though the available secondary materials do touch upon
the aspect of Harlem, mostly in the historical context, none of them
have Harlem as the specific focus of their study.

A classic "thriller of manners" (Bailey 54) by "one of the brightest
lights of the Harlem Renaissance" (Deutsch 82), Rudolph Fisher's *The
Conjure Man Dies* creates a niche for itself. With its eccentric storyline and involvement of multiple detectives for a supposed crime
which is a misjudgment, the novel boasts of a peculiar and unique
structure. This aspect resurfaces as noted by Maria Balshaw, who
claims that *The Conjure Man Dies* is one of the most overlooked texts
of the era because "there seems so little context for understanding an
African American detective novel in this period; perhaps more because its 'inherent variety' of form makes it a difficult text to classify
or respond to" (38). In *The Afro-American Novel and Its Tradition*,
Bernard Bell notes that it is a hybrid work, combining the classical
model of S.S. Van Dine and the realistic mode of Dashiell Hammett
(140), and further notes, "structurally and stylistically, *The Conjure-Man Dies* is an incongruous combination of mystery and low
comedy" (141). Also, this aspect of hybridity is referenced by Wintz
and Finkelman when they note that Fisher's *The Conjure Man Dies*
amalgamates "elements of classic detective stories such as the locked-
room mystery and the police procedural" along with the elements
representative and associated with "the African American vernacular,
urban rituals, and contemporary social issues" (247).

Set during the Harlem Renaissance, the geographical locale of
New York vis-à-vis Harlem becomes prominent. Historical docu-
mentation of the era records that the Black population from various
southern states migrated to the northern states of the USA, obviously because of the racial identity, economics and the laws governing
the American South. That argument finds its way in the writings of
Alain Locke and the militant ideology of W.E.B. Du Bois. Dan S.
Green and Edwin D. Driver note that Du Bois himself had predicted,
"'Unless the race conflict there is so adjusted as to leave the negroes

a contented, industrious people, they are going to migrate here and there. And into the large cities will pour in increasing numbers the competent and the incompetent, the industrious and the lazy, the law-abiding and the criminal'" (as qtd. in Green and Driver 143). Later scholars like Carla L. Peterson confirm the observation and in her genealogical study, she agrees with Alain Locke and W.E.B. Du Bois and notes, "before Harlem, there was New York" (18), making the point that New York City had a significant Black population from its founding, long before there was a place and a culture associated with the name "Harlem." She further explains that the reason for the shift in population from the South to the North varied "from vagrancy and idle tourism to escape from Jim Crow laws in the South and hope for a better life in the big city" (18-19). In the larger context of *The Conjure Man Dies*, Dennis Poupard opines, "Fisher was one of the first 'New Negro' writers to satirize both black and white society as he explored the serious problems of the newly-migrated black southerner in Harlem, examining interracial and intraracial prejudices and the conflict between traditional and modern mores" (202). With the Black population migrating from the American South to the American North, there was a noticeable and substantial increase in the customs and practices more associated with the continent of Africa in the North, whose presence was bound to be felt across Harlem. The setting of the novel reverberates with a similar situation, where Frimbo the protagonist practices his art of deduction (mostly from what his clients reveal about themselves to him, as he expounds to Dr. Archer) and makes his living as a conjurer, though he claims himself to be a psychist.

I. Harlem as a Geo-Political Space

It becomes imperative to explore Harlem as a physical space, as well as a social space, within the city of New York. *The Conjure Man Dies* begins and ends in the streets of Harlem. While the opening lines of the novel boast of the salient features and characteristics of Harlem, vying for a vivid description, the ending of the novel deals with the closure of the case of the conjurer's murder, Jinx, being freed as a suspect in the crime, and the two friends, Bubber and Jinx, wandering off down Seventh Avenue. This aspect of Harlem as a physical space is noted by Monique M. Taylor, who observes, "Rudolph Fisher, a writer who saw himself as an 'interpreter' of Harlem, made use of Harlem as a physical space to explore the contradictions of black American life brought about by the great migration" (14).

Harlem's Seventh Avenue is a gleeful space and this space is sharply contrasted to the "black Harlem" associated with "dark chill silent side streets" (4), where the novel's narrator notes, "but all of black Harlem was not thus gay and bright" (4). This is the location that sustains the psychist-cum-conjurer, N'Gana Frimbo, and Dr. John Archer. Craftily, the exact location of Frimbo's house within the city of New York is observed by Bubber who, while calling the police observes,

> Operator – gimme the station – quick …. Pennsylvania? No ma'am - New York – Harlem – listen, lady, not railroad. Police. Please, ma'am…. Hello – hey – send a flock o' cops around here – Frimbo's – the fortune teller's – yea – Thirteen West 130th- yea- somebody done put that thing on him! (12)

Both Frimbo and Dr. John Archer are the occupants of the same street, with Archer, "dwelling directly opposite" (5) the conjurer. From the very beginning, the locale is defined by its inherent ominousness in contrast to the joyful side of Harlem.

The building on 130th Street, east of Lenox Avenue, which houses the central character of the novel, the psychist N'Gana Frimbo, is a dimly lit building with a mood of ominous foreboding, and the narrative voice notes, "about the place hovered an oppressive silence, as if those who entered here were warned beforehand not to speak above a whisper" (4). Moreover, Frimbo's consultation room has been called a "'queer place. Dark as sin'" (19). Additionally, the caretaker of the building, Mr. Crouch, runs his funeral parlor downstairs and the space reeks of darkness, death, and horror. This claim is further supported by one of the major personas of the novel, Jinx Jenkins, who ironically is a suspect initially, and later acts like a detective. Jinx states that Frimbo's place is more horrifying than a graveyard and observes, "'Graveyard's a playground side o' this'" (13). This specific space within New York City is home to the darker side of human civilization, with conflict between street gangs leading to street killings, making Bubber Brown observe, "'This Harlem is jes' too bad'" (192).

Moreover, this part of Harlem is largely devoid of any economic affluence, and this becomes clear by the description of the residents. The novel is set in the time of the Great Depression. The action takes place in the month of February, and the third person omniscient narrative voice notes that in general, the geopolitical space is full of "women with complexions from cream to black coffee and with costumes, individually and collectively, running the range of the rainbow, the men with derbies, canes, high collars, spats, and a dignity peculiar to doormen, chauffeurs, and headwaiters" (186). While there are some practitioners of professions, most of the men described in the setting are employed as menial workers, while joblessness haunts youths like Bubber and Jinx.

Additionally, it is a space where no white men venture; it lies outside the purview of the white and dominant America, and through the composition of the investigating team (composed of Dart and his subordinates) that engages with the apparent murder of the conjure man, Frimbo, it is clear that the State wants the African American faction occupying Harlem, the city within the city, to maintain their homogeneous identities. The narrative voice is blatantly critical of the State and its openly racist actions, and observes,

> As if the city administration had wished to leave no doubt in the public mind as to its intention in the matter, they had chosen, in him, a man who could not have been under any circumstances mistaken for aught but a Negro; or perhaps, as Dart's intimates insisted, they had chosen him because his generously pigmented skin rendered him invisible in the dark, a conceivably great advantage to a detective who did most of his work at night. (14)

Also, later, when Dart realizes that more policemen are required for the ongoing investigation, he orders, "'send me four more men – doesn't matter who'" (19). His words again give the impression that probably the white policemen within the police force are reluctant to work under the Black police detective, Dart. This curious and total absence of the white faction in the whole novel can be viewed as gross indifference and negligence of the white faction toward the African American populace.

The geographical location of the novel remains constant and all the actions take place either in the building where the presumed dead body of the famous occultist Frimbo is found or near it, from where a few suspects, Spider Webb and Doty Hicks, are taken in to be questioned by the police. Additionally, there are a few more streets and landmarks of Harlem that are mentioned, like the Roosevelt Theatre, which is playing *Murder Between Drinks* (296) and the iconic and now demolished Lafayette Theatre, where Bubber has his first commercial success as a private investigator (50). This kind of information enriches the narrative structure by giving it a realistic grounding, along with locating the novel in a space distinct from the larger white American population.

Importantly, Harlem acts as space where almost all the major characters get the chance to play the role of an investigator. The NYPD send Detective Dart and his assistants to solve the apparent murder of Frimbo and, from the very beginning, Dr. John Archer acts as a close associate of the State-backed investigator, Dart. The two of them form a separate investigating team, where no one acts as the sidekick as per the structure of traditional detective stories. Fisher's *The Conjure Man Dies* has four detectives to solve the mystery of the assumed murder of Frimbo, with Frimbo himself a detective. Dr. Archer acts as a detective, and at one point he notes about himself, "'all my training and all my activities are those of a detective. The criminal I chase is as prime a rascal as you'll ever find – assailant, thief, murderer – disease. In each case I get, it's my job to track disease down, identify it, and arrest it. What else is diagnosis and treatment?'" (209). Bailey refers to him as "an erudite amateur detective" (54). Curiously, the protagonist Frimbo himself acts as a detective, trying to solve his own murder, a charge which later is reduced down to attempt to murder. Moreover, Bubber Brown with his highly sexist and ridiculous business plan (he believes that women whose husbands are employed and are seldom home are not morally upright) is self-employed as a "family detective" (48), that is, a private investigator, and he also contributes to the investigation by acting as an informer and saving his friend Jinx from jail; at one point he is called "Sherlock" by Jinx (196).

Lastly, a close study of the novel reveals that objectively there is a gradual thematic elevation of Harlem. From a space largely confined by its geographical and racial underpinnings, eventually Harlem becomes a part of the self-consciousness for the characters involved in the narrative thrust of the novel. The ground of commonality shared by the residents of Harlem lies in their location on the margins of the mainstream—white—American society. This gradual marginalization of the residents leads to a sense of belonging and unity among them. This unification is observed within the Black quarters of Harlem, a stronghold of the African American settlers. It seems that the Black population is turned inward by the idea of white American's interference. It becomes clear when Dr. Archer and detective Dart are linked together. While Dart is elated at the prospect of working with Dr. Archer, so does Dr. Archer want Dart and his team to get the credit and the ensuing recognition for solving the case. On the one hand, while Dart says, "All right, doc. It's irregular, of course, but I believe it's the best way. And I'd rather work with you than—some others'" (184-185); on the other hand, Dr. Archer also celebrates Dart's appointment in Frimbo's case, and says, "'I'm glad you're on this one. It'll take a little active cerebration'" (15), and later notes, "'I'd like to see you and the local boys get the credit for this whole thing – not a lot of Philistines from downtown'" (207-208). Similarly, this kind of unity is visible between Bubber and Jinx as well. Bubber is really concerned about his friend Jinx, proves his innocence and ensures that Jinx is freed by the law. Yet, it is also to be noted that, in spite of the oneness and unity, there is division even within this society. A close look at the text reveals that the division results not directly from differences of skin color, but on whether one identifies as African or African American (or predominately American).

II. Harlem as a racial space

Though Robert L. Southgate notes that "there is no mention of the issue of race or race problems in the entire novel: what is presented is a murder mystery along the lines of S.S. Van Dine's Philo Vance stories…." (60), a close reading of the text and the ensuing textual analysis proves otherwise. The geopolitical space of Harlem encompasses a population very much concerned with racial issues. The inhabitants of the immediate neighborhood are members of the African American community, and they hold certain racial prejudices themselves, and the less fortunate ones among them are subjected to racial discrimination and stigmatization. It appears that with the unending and ongoing reality of racial subjugation, the African American community has gradually prioritized a desire for lighter skin, and the spatial reality of Harlem attempts to implement this desire in their lives, as conveyed and manifested through these characters. Within the community members are extremely conscious of their skin color. This aspect is aptly captured by the owner of Frimbo's building, Mr. Crouch, in the larger context of his macabre role as beautician in his funeral parlor. Mr. Crouch is an expert in embalming dead bodies and he notes, "'we can make the dark ones bright and the bright ones lighter—that seems to be the ambition in this community'" (91). This color obsession is a continual theme explored in African American detective fiction. Mr. Crouch's description of the community's "ambition" is well reflected in contemporary African American writer, Barbara Neely's detective Blanche White, a single mother, working as a helper in white households. She also regrets the color obsession and blatantly criticizes the general populace as,

> Everybody in the country got color on the brain—white folks trying to brown themselves up and looking down on everything that ain't white at the same time; black folks puttin' each other down for being too black; brown folks trying to make sure nobody mistakes them for black; yellow folks trying to convince themselves they're white. (8-9)

This continued obsession regarding skin color can be partly attributed to the space. Though the concerned space where Fisher's novel is set is essentially dominated by African Americans, Harlem is an integral part of New York, a city dominated by white Americans in the nineteen thirties. It is the dominant white faction who define the norms of desirability, and as a result the African American community at large, as Fisher depicts it, desire to be of lighter shade. This claim can be substantiated by Dr. Archer himself, who is "'almost white,'" while Frimbo on the other hand is "'almost black'" (230).

As the novel depicts, N'Gana Frimbo is an intelligent individual from Buwongo with a Bachelor's degree from Harvard. Though due to the nature of his occupation he is rendered as one of the "conjure-men in Harlem" (82), Frimbo has "'built himself up quite a following here in Harlem – at least he always had plenty of people in here at night'" (86). A trickster, but a keen observer of human nature who is popular amongst the locals, Frimbo is smart enough to fool a practicing physician like Dr. Archer into believing that it is possible to challenge Western medical science, making Dr. Archer exclaim, "apparently your serum agglutinates its own cells. But that's impossible. One part of your blood couldn't destroy another – and you remain alive'" (266). Through his tricks and the capabilities of a con-man, Frimbo can confuse Dr. Archer who, in his analysis, declares Frimbo to be paranoic. But even Dr. Archer has to admit that it must be Frimbo's experience of racism, racial discrimination, and ensuing oppression when he came to America to gain a Western education that must have rendered him paranoic (259). As reported by Dr. Dart, during his attempt at entrance examinations, Frimbo "had acquired a bitter prejudice against the dominant race that had seemed to be opposing his purpose. Many episodes had fostered this bitterness, making it the more acute in one accustomed to absolute authority and domination" (229). In Emad Mirmotahari's understanding, the "city within a city," Harlem, comprises two subgroups within the African American community, and Frimbo is a racial victim at the hands of the Black Americans. Mirmotahari notes, "in Harlem, Frimbo experiences racism of a peculiar kind, not from white Europeans (white characters are practically absent, though whiteness is a spectral ideological super-structure), but from black Americans, a powerful statement on the internal paradoxes of diaspora" (274).

In *Talking About Detective Fiction*, P.D James remarks that it is difficult for detective fiction to flourish in the absence of an organized system of law (6). Within the novel, the policemen who engage in the investigation process are all African American, and are a part of the New York City Police Department, which is shown to be white-dominated, and out of them only ten "Negro members" have been "promoted from the rank of patrolman to that of detective" (14). The Black detective Perry Dart, who "represents a new era in the criminal justice system" (Brown 93), is one of the finest and first ranked detectives in the department, but there are racist insinuations in the narrator's description: Dart has been chosen for Frimbo's case as "his generously pigmented skin rendered him invisible in the dark, a conceivably great advantage to a detective who did most of his work at night" (14). That brings us to the curious structure of the State-backed police system. A close reading of the text reveals that there is not a single white American in the whole novel, and probably Dr. John Archer is the only persona with a lighter complexion, as, at one point, Frimbo notes to Dr. Archer, "'you are almost white. I am almost black'" (230). This aspect is further dealt with subtly by the police department in which the subservient party is constantly under the watchful eyes of the master. Interestingly, the color-obsessed society and the setting are clearly relevant in the professional sphere as well. Of Dart's four assistants, Day, Green, Johnson, and Brady, the narrative voice observes "... one black, two brown, and one yellow" (15), pointing toward a racist workplace where white policemen are not supposed to work under any non-white superiors or take orders from them. Later, this aspect of the racist setup within the police force is again revealed by one of the ladies who was present in the building when Frimbo was allegedly murdered. When questioned by Detective Dart, the lady in question, Mrs. Snead, is not ready to accept that there are Black detectives within the police department. She is dismayed at being questioned by such a detective, and observes, "'police detective? 'Tain't so. They don't have no black detectives'" (79). The racial setting is further confirmed by Emad Mirmotahari as he notes, "Fisher's novel, however, ultimately shows that the African is foreign and even 'other' to black Americans, a people that perceive Africans not as kith and kin, but through the same colonial optics that shaped nineteenth- to mid-twentieth-century European perceptions of Africans" (269). The aspect of "other" has been further taken up in *Post-Colonial Studies: The Key Concepts*, by Bill Ashcroft, Gareth Griffiths, and Helen Tiffin, who note at one point, "In general terms, the 'other' is anyone who is separate from one's self. The existence of others is crucial in defining what is 'normal' and in locating one's own place in the world" (154).

Though there is no direct reference to racist slurs that Bubber receives from the dominant white Americans, yet he is taken aback at being referred to as "Mr.," and it is revealed that he has not been referred to as "Mr." six times in twenty-six years (46). It is also to be noted that initially Bubber was a menial worker whose work was "'hauling ashes for the city'" (196), as described by Jinx. It is possible that he might have been working in white neighborhoods where he would never have been referred to as "Mr." The mean streets of New York along with its openly racist structure are reflected in the professional sphere as well, as proven by one of Frimbo's clients, Easley Jones, who points out indirectly that the mainstream American workspace is by and large controlled by powerful white Americans, and most of the African Americans being employed by the whites are meant for menial work. About his own profession of being a porter, he laments, "'now what else do the Pullman Company put n[------] on trains for?'" (126).

In Harlem, the use of racial slurs is an integral part of everyday practice. The narrative voice notes at one instance that Bubber is constantly racially abused by the other residents in his vicinity and that the "acquaintances standing in entrances or passing him by offered the genial insults which were characteristic Harlem greetings" (187). Moreover, these general characteristics of the Black population of Harlem are comically captured by two of the major characters of the novel, Bubber Brown and Jinx Jenkins. These two friends are commonly found insulting each other in a congenial and jovial mood, a tone which negates the openly voiced racial slurs. In this context, it can be argued that Harlem as a space is the realization of hopelessness. The kind of wordplay used by the Harlemites of Fisher's novel might be taken as a sign that they are helpless and hopeless and that they have gradually internalized self-hatred to an extent where they remain unaffected by the racial slurs.

Lastly, it is imperative to locate the women of Fisher's novel within the rubric of gender and race. The novel deals with fewer women characters. The main plot of the novel refers to the pious lady, Mrs. Aramintha Snead, and Mrs. Crouch, who were present during the time of the crime. Additionally, there is just a passing reference to Doty Hicks' unnamed sister-in-law, the "'show-gal,'" who "'met up with some guy with more sugar'" (112), and is absurdly accused of killing Doty's brother. Among the women characters, the most important is Martha Crouch, the landlady, and as is later revealed, Frimbo's secret lover.

It is Mrs. Martha Crouch, who has received some attention in the work of Charles Scruggs. In a comparative study of Nella Larsen and Rudolph Fisher, Scruggs notes that in Fisher's The Conjure Man Dies, the primary investigation required is more than mere "rational analysis" (or ratiocination as propounded by the founding father of the genre, Edgar Allan Poe). He argues that almost in the guise of a comic intonation, the clue required to solve the crime lies in the "song about sexual desire heard daily on Harlem's streets" (155). He proves his point by noting the attempt by Dr. Archer (who according to him is based on the classical detective Sherlock Holmes) and Detective Perry Dart "to solve the crime of Frimbo's 'murder' through ratiocination, empirical evidence, and the scientific method" (163). He further adds, "so absorbed are they in their analysis of clues that they overlook the obvious" (163). The obvious in this context is the sexual liaison between Mrs. Crouch and Frimbo, the source of the crime and the reason for two murders, that of Frimbo's doppelganger cock-eyed servant, and Frimbo himself. Loosely, it seems that Mrs. Crouch is to be blamed for the ensuing bloodshed. It is in the light of this discussion that Mrs. Crouch gains literary attention, whereby her character is by and large portrayed negatively, and she is limited to the stereotype of a woman characterized by sexual infidelity.

In Fisher's The Conjure Man Dies, the women are essentially helpless within their situational realities. Mrs. Snead is a victim of domestic violence and is physically abused by her drunkard husband, Jake. The callous religious authorities pacify and supply her with impractical and illogical solutions. Within the mean streets of Harlem, the landlady, Mrs. Crouch, is not to be trusted with collecting rents from her tenants after sunset, with Dart questioning, "'isn't that rather a dangerous occupation for a woman? Carrying money about?'" (87). Later, it is absurdly explained that it is out of her physical inability to bear children and her resulting boredom that the landlady engages in the rent collection work as a way of keeping herself busy. Lastly, clients like Easley Jones visit Frimbo to check on his wife's fidelity, since he fears that his physical absence due to the nature of his work may lure his wife into infidelity. Coincidentally, Easley Jones' reason for visiting a psychist is the same as Bubber's reason for being self-employed as a family detective as Bubber believes that men who are often away for work have wives likely to be unfaithful; therefore, he tries to befriend Easley Jones whom he considers as a potential customer, as he is mostly away on work related travels. At one point, Bubber notes that, "'railroad men is the most back-bitten bozos in the world'" (106). Thus, two different kinds of occupations for the males validate themselves based on the assumed infidelity commonly associated with the women. The number of women in the novel is limited, but through nuanced analysis, it becomes clear that Fisher's Harlem represses its women and that, within the oppressed and the marginalized African American community, the Black women are doubly marginalized and further pushed towards the periphery by Black men.

III. Harlem as the Melting Pot of the Orient and the Occident

A close reading of the novel reveals that though the novel boasts an ensemble group of Black characters, the characters are roughly divided into two major factions. The first group chiefly made up of Dr. Archer, Detective Dart, and Bubber Brown consider themselves Americans (the Occidentals) and view the second group consisting of Frimbo and his servant N'Ogo (the Orientals) as definitely not a part of their American society. Interestingly, both the groups are staunch in their beliefs and it is only the pious lady, Mrs. Aramintha Snead, who agrees that though she is an American at present, she originally hails from Savannah, Georgia (80), demonstrating in a humorous manner an internal division between New York, as America, and Georgia, in the American South, as not-America. Interestingly, parallel to the ongoing clash between Dr. Archer and Frimbo, there is a constant playful dispute between Bubber and Jinx. While Jinx is mostly silent due to his nature, garrulous Bubber frequently and playfully insults and tags his friend Jinx as a primitive African. When Bubber tells Jinx, "'You ought to be back in Africa with the other dumb boogies'" (34), Jinx responds, "'African boogies ain't dumb... They jes' dark'" (34). Such remarks between the characters show that while both the Americans and the Africans share a skin tone, the idea of "African-ness" is, in the Black American mind, strongly associated with the primitive and the non-Western.

Within the first group, both Dr. Archer and Dart are representatives of the Occidental knowledge system, while Frimbo, in spite of his training within the Western academy, is the Oriental representative. There is a continuous and conscious attempt to pin Frimbo to the native Africa, both by Dr. Archer and Dart, despite Frimbo's education in a "mission school in Liberia" and an American university (229). To begin with, Dr. Archer attempts to establish Frimbo's identity by dissecting Frimbo's name: "'This sounds definitely African to me. Lots of them have that N'. The 'Frimbo' suggests it, too – mumbo – jumbo – sambo–'" (27). Besides, as long as Frimbo is assumed to be dead, Dr. Archer notes about Frimbo's profession, "'Probably a better racket than medicine in this community'" (27), which proves that for Dr. Archer, "'this community'" is definitely not Frimbo's community; this is further exposed when he tags Frimbo as a "'native African, a Harvard graduate, a student of philosophy—and a sorcerer'" (27-28). While for Dr. Archer, Frimbo is an "apparent charlatan" (176), detective Dart internally believes that Frimbo is "a master of the power of darkness" (80), and essentially an outsider, who may evade Harlem and "'be back in Bunghola, or wherever he hails from, by then'" (204). Dart is a proud "Harlemite" and knows the quarters of Harlem thoroughly. As a Black man himself, Dart shows that he has internalized certain stereotypes about the shared heritage of Africans and African Americans when, while studying blood samples, Dart sees "'lot of little reddish dots'" not moving. He focuses upon the blood cells' lack of motion, and announces, "'Must be Negro blood'" (202-203) implying that Negroes are essentially lazy. Like Bubber's playful insults to Jinx, this painful stereotype is offered with a "grin[]" and accepted as a "'jest'" by Archer (203).

Frimbo is the "'African mystic'" (154) who on his part also firmly establishes himself as a representative of the Orient. To Dr. Archer he reasserts, "'I am an African native'" (215), and the narrative voice notes, "There was a pride in the statement that was almost affront" (215). Frimbo also remarks that their (Dr. Archer's and his own) cultural affiliations are different, and for him understanding urban space is as difficult as it is for Dr. Archer to comprehend bush/tribal space. He tells Dr. Archer, "'the bush would be a challenge to all your resources. The city is a similar challenge to mine'" (216). Furthermore, enhancing the mysticism associated with the Orient, Frimbo tells Jinx,

> For, in addition to the things that can be learned by anyone, Frimbo inherits the bequest of a hundred centuries, handed from son to son through four hundred unbroken generations of Buwongo kings. It is a profound and dangerous secret, my friend, a secret my fathers knew when the kings of the Nile still thought human flesh a delicacy. (69)

Regarding his own observation, it is to be noticed that he uses the term "'fathers,'" alluding to his forefathers, thereby trying to establish a direct link between his present location and his cultural origin. This reference to the father-line reverberates later through Frimbo's association and understanding of the gonad and its cultural affiliations. Also, regarding his own profession, he tells Dr. Archer, "'I can study a person's face and tell his past, present, and future'" (226), and, later, he adds, "'I tell you in all seriousness that here, in a world of rigidly determined causes and effects, Frimbo is free—as free as a being of another order'" (228). His explanation of himself as belonging to a different realm reinforces his representation of the Oriental knowledge system.

Frimbo's Oriental adherence is further confirmed through the figure of his father, the head of the tribe, who was, in the story told by Frimbo to Archer, injured during a hunting expedition. His society is essentially tribal, where, according to the existing practice of primogeniture, Frimbo was supposed to fill in his father's shoes. Lastly, through the interplay of culture and the resulting customs there is the oppositional reality of Frimbo and Dr. Archer. Whereas Dr. Archer, though he is not religious himself, is associated with Christianity, Frimbo is essentially associated with a tribe and its rituals. Frimbo reiterates the politics of Western construction of the savage and the heathen, and regarding his doppelganger servant he says, "'His distinguished name, had he not been a heathen and a savage – was N'Ogo'" (304). It becomes clear that Frimbo also considers that he is in foreign world. Regarding his royal duties toward his subjects, he notes that his duties vary in their nature, in "'my own land'" and "'here in yours'" (305).

Analyzing the politics of the construction of the Orient, Richard V. Francaviglia notes that in the contemporary world, it is difficult to define the Orient, as it is any place geographically located in the east. The Orient in itself is a European construction and the politics associated with it have been expounded by Edward Said in one of the cornerstone texts of the twentieth century, *Orientalism* (6). He goes on to state, "The Orient, of course, is as much a state of mind as an actual place" (7). This notion is re-iterated by Clare Corbould, who writes, "in the words of Howard University philosopher Alain Locke, the northern Manhattan neighborhood is 'the *Mecca* [emphasis added] of the New Negro'" (10). Taking this cue a step further, with an even better and appropriate observation, Stephen Soitos notes, "Rudolph Fisher, as a Harlem Renaissance writer, recognized that Harlem was a 'city within a city,' with its own African American value systems and culture" (94). Fisher's Harlem therefore is a space which accommodates the Orient, allows cultures to mix, where the "other" or the African Americans try to uphold their belief systems by practicing their cultural beliefs.

Harlem as a space acts as the melting pot of cultures. It is a space where a confluence of the Occidental and Oriental knowledge systems occurs. Frimbo, a representative of the Oriental knowledge system, is pitted against Dr. John Archer, who in turn represents the Occidental knowledge system and the investigation team consisting of Detective Dart and the helping investigators. Though for the common residents of Harlem, Frimbo might be a conjure man, he is well versed in Western philosophy. This becomes evident when, in Frimbo's apartment, Dr. Archer, "noted such titles as Tankard's *Determinism and Fatalism, a Critical Contrast*, Bostwick's *The Concept of Inevitability*, Preem's *Cause and Effect*, Dassault's *The Science of History*, and Fairclough's *The Philosophical Basis of Destiny*" (27). The shrouded and mysterious nature of Frimbo's work makes Dr. Archer claim that "'this man was no ordinary fakir'" (26). Later in the novel, when Dr. Archer and Frimbo engage in philosophical discussions, Dr. Archer notes to Frimbo, "'I thought you were a mystic, not a mechanist'" (214). Reiterating Dr. Archer's claim, Frimbo himself assures Archer that he is not a seer at all, and though he impresses Dr. Archer with his predictions, he explains, "'you told me all that in the few words you spoke. I filled in the gaps, that is all. I have done more with less. It is my livelihood'" (225). This raises the possibility that Frimbo might be rational and scientific in orientation (something closely associated with the Occident), yet this paper has shown that Frimbo is a staunch Orientalist. So, where do Frimbo and Dr. Archer lie between the two oppositional ideas of Orient and Occident?

Now, it is to be kept in mind that while Frimbo was trained in the West and therefore comprises both the Occidental and the Oriental knowledge systems (which is his cultural material), Dr. Archer, on the other hand, is solely trained and educated in the Occidental knowledge system. Therefore, it is easier to locate Dr. Archer, as his mystic or the Oriental part is totally absent (we are not even sure about his religiousness, in spite of his overtly religious father, since no proof can be found in the text), while for Frimbo it is slightly complicated. It may appear that he uses Occidental knowledge to make his living; as far as his occupation is concerned, no direct evidence of such possibility is confirmed in the text, though he explains to Archer that his seemingly mystical abilities are "'merely practiced observation to the degree of great proficiency'" (225). Though it may appear that having femurs on display is a sign of scientific orientation, gradually it becomes clear that the femurs have been stripped of their scientific significance and are merely decorative pieces now, as they have become "two clubs with the silver tips" (83), and later, it is revealed that these "clubs" are kept at the opposite ends of the "mantelpiece" (128), openly visible to his clients. Similarly, though Dr. Archer notices, "'He has chemistry apparatus that a physician's lab would never need except for research, and few practicing physicians have time for that kind of research'" (197), we really do not find any evidence of Frimbo engaging in any scientific experiments. Rather, he uses fundamental knowledge of Western science to accomplish his culturally defined duties. For instance, though the investigating team is shocked by the amount of electricity he uses, it becomes clear that he needs electricity to operate the lift (where he successfully hides the dead body of his servant), and for the blinding lights that he needs in his consultation room. Similarly, his uses of laboratory equipment are confined to storing the harvested organs of people that he later uses to fulfill his cultural duties. Also, it can be noted that his understanding of the gonads is totally unscientific and devoid of any rational idea. Instead of debunking Oriental superstition with the help of Occidental science (as is expected from an individual trained in Occidental rationalism), he attempts to link the two. His understanding of the gonad, and the importance of the gonad in human lives is stated as,

> The germplasm, of which the gonad is the only existing sample, is the unbroken heritage of the past. It is protoplasm which has been continuously maintained throughout thousands of generations. It's the only vital matter which goes back in a continuous line to the remotest origins of the organism. It is therefore the only matter which brings into the present every influence which the past has imprinted upon life. It is the epitome of the past. He who can learn its use can be master of his past. And he who can master his past – that man is free. (269)

Lastly, one question remains unanswered regarding his training/education in the Occidental West. It is clear that he is a Harvard graduate, but his major subject of study remains shrouded in mystery. This seemingly unimportant point gains momentum once we ask how much of Occidental education/training is enough to be reflected in one's practices? Apart from the fact that his understanding of science is basic, the books that are found in his apartment are of Western philosophy. Assuming that his training is in the field of philosophy, rather than science, it can be safely concluded that his mechanistic/Occidental part is less developed than the Oriental counterpart, an argument which has been substantiated by Frimbo himself, when he claims that absolute belief in anything "'undemonstrable'" is mysticism (214).

As stated earlier, it becomes evident that through the image of "fakir," "mystic," and "seer," there is a constant and conscious attempt to locate Frimbo within the Oriental knowledge system. More importantly, Frimbo's paraphernalia is depicted as Oriental in nature and that aspect is well reflected within the physical dimensions he inhabits. His bedchamber is covered with a Chinese rug and consists of a four-poster intricately carved mahogany bed, settee, and smoking stand (24). Even his chamber is shaped like an "Arab tent" (38). Moreover, articles like human femurs and "male sex glands" are to be found in his apartment (41). Also, Frimbo's blackout while reading Jinx's face, and the realization that his end is near can be considered as a mysterious occasion for the Occidentals. Additionally, it is obvious that both Frimbo and his clients or his followers are occultists in nature. The general public favoring Frimbo is superstitious, unscientific, and irrational in their orientation. Frimbo is almost a demigod. He is believed to be the controller of life and death, favoring some while wrecking others. It is widely rumored that he can put spells on people, both to kill them (Doty's ailing brother) or to save them (Susan Gassoway's son, Lem) and, therefore, one of Frimbo's clients, Doty, attempts to kill him by reversing Frimbo's alleged death spell (113), though Frimbo himself explains by remarking that, "'I am no caster of spells. I am a psychist – a kind of psychologist'" (114). Needless to say, psychology is a part of a Western knowledge system based on the precepts of Western rationalism, but we don't find any direct evidence of the same. Rather, his occupation defies any Western knowledge system. He is the master of the Oriental knowledge system, and when he comes back to life from the realm of death, he explains that he was in a state of "suspended animation," (171) an unrealistic explanation, unacceptable to the rationalized minds of the modern-day readers, while he exclaims,

> More exactly, I was wholly immune to activities of the immediate present, for I had projected my mind into the future – that gentleman's future – Mr. Jenkins'. During that period I was assaulted – murderously. Physically, I was murdered. Mentally I could not be, because mentally I was elsewhere. Do you see? (171)

This irrational explanation leads to a conflict between Dr. Archer and Frimbo and, when Frimbo revitalizes himself from the state of death, since Dr. Archer was the one to pronounce Frimbo as dead, his capabilities and the whole parameters of Western, scientific, rational knowledge system are jeopardized. Frimbo, the representative of the Oriental world, is well aware of it. At Frimbo's resurrection from death, while Bubber claims, "'he done done a Lazarus!'" (170), Frimbo takes a jibe at the doctor of the Occidental half, questions the Western knowledge system as a whole, and notes, "'Dr. Archer who pronounced me dead, will naturally be most reluctant to identify me with the corpse since the implication would be that he had been mistaken in his original pronouncement'" (173-174).

To sum up, while Dr. Archer is totally scientific and can easily be categorized as a staunch Occidental, Frimbo is the absolute Oriental; and yet his practice of the Oriental knowledge system has some tinge of Occidental, Western rationalism. This becomes evident when Frimbo accepts that he had succeeded in devising a mathematical formula to win policy money, incurring the wrath of notorious policy makers (307).

In the novel, Harlem becomes the fertile ground where two cultures meet. Though Frimbo is a member of African royalty, where his younger brother rules the land in his absence, he is the bridge between his culture and the Western culture, as he "…. had departed for America to acquire knowledge of Western Civilization…" (229), and he has successfully finished his Western education. At the same time, there is a conscious juxtaposition between his world and that of Dr. Archer. The festival of Malindo, described as the "'feast of pro-creation,'" where, "'slim naked girls'" are objects of amusement (221), is in stark contrast to Dr. John Archer's youth, which is "'so utterly different'" along with the associated memory of the strawberry festival in Archer's father's church (224). This raises the probability that if Dr. Archer was raised in a religious family in which his father was a church minister, he might have been raised in the tradition of the irrational, which he balanced out with his education in the rational field of medicine. But such a contention is problematic, once a few factors are taken into consideration. First, whereas Frimbo presents a vivid, detailed and well-expressed description of Malindo, Dr. Ar-cher's strawberry festival is merely a passing reference, which in itself points at the possibility that the young Archer was not influenced by either his father's profession or by the festival itself. Second, nowhere in the text is Archer presented as a religious man. He is the absolute rationalist, who believes and practices science. Third, in Dr. Archer's story, the focus is more on the financial struggle regarding the ex-pense of studying medicine. Lastly, just like Frimbo's understanding of science is limited and lesser than that of Dr. Archer, Dr. Archer's understanding of philosophy is much less than Frimbo's, obviously owing to their different professional training. To conclude, since readers are not provided with enough information about the rela-tionship between Dr. Archer and his father, assuming that he balanc-es out rational science with his father's tradition of irrational religion is an unnecessary speculation.

Watson writes, "In his literary writing, Fisher consistently depict-ed the complexities of Black life, particularly the myriad beliefs and manners that attended it" (168). The focal point of cultural analo-gy lies in the depiction of culture between Frimbo and Dr. Archer. Though time and again, the barbarity of the native African culture is portrayed, yet as the narrative thrust suggests, it is the cultural dictum (whereby the chief of the tribe, being the carrier of State secrets is to be protected from physical dangers) that finally reveals the identity of the murderer. For Frimbo and his tradition (which is barbaric according to the dictums of the Western knowledge system), the tradition of the "rite of the gonad," which has been interpreted by Gosselin as Fisher's way of parodying Freud (616), defines one's cultural identity and connects with one's past, where the gonad is deemed and revered as the "'unbroken heritage of the past'" (269), while for the Westernized and rational Dr. Archer, it is an act of perilous barbarity.

In *Postcolonial Theory: A Critical Introduction*, Leela Gandhi notes that even in the current global discourse, there is an ongoing trend of rendering non-Western knowledge and culture as the "other" due to the non-conformity of the Oriental knowledge system to the constructed normative of the Occident (ix-x). The conjurer-cum-psychist Frimbo's intelligence and belief system are misunderstood and misinterpreted by Dr. Archer, who terms Malindo –the feast of procreation–as a "'dangerous ceremony'" (223), and it is eventually rumored that Frimbo treats himself with testicular extract periodically (291), which can be summed up as an act of "hierarchical grouping and the erroneous assumptions of folk knowledge that accompany it" (Watson 173). Regarding this assumption, Dr. Archer tells Dart that "'[s]ex gland deficiency can be helped by such treatment, so perhaps a normal person would become, in some respects, oversexed'" (291). This hyper-sexuality that Frimbo is associated with again redirects him towards the realm of primitivism and linked Orientalism.

Moreover, in Harlem, where these two cultures amalgamate, the civilized system of properly revering the dead and following the customs of the burial of the dead (as adhered to by the followers of Abrahamic religions) is starkly contrasted by Frimbo's tribal custom, which involves the illegal act of burning the mortal remains secretly (304), as luckily discovered by Bubber Brown in the basement of Frimbo's building while Bubber is fleeing from a goon of Harlem. Yet, it should be kept in mind that within this conflict of culture there is no clear winner, and the admiration and respect that Dr. Archer evinces for Frimbo is worth remembering. Within this space, racial identity is overshadowed by intellectual capacity, and Dr. Archer is awed by Frimbo's. Both of them hold each other in high esteem. At the same time, it can also be observed that for Frimbo's cock-eyed servant, N'Ogo, it is an honor to be able to use the title of his king (N'Gana Frimbo,) and he lays down his life to save the life of his king, Frimbo. Since Frimbo's servant dies saving his life, according to the practices of his culture, N'Ogo's sex glands must be preserved, and that explains the sexual organs at his place (306-307). Ultimately, Frimbo risks his own life and his attempt to ascertain the identity of the killer proves fatal for him. But native African Frimbo and his cultural adherence, in that he sacrifices his own life for his servant, in effect questions the white Western power hierarchy , along with re-establishing and redefining the notion of kingship and kinship.

Concluding Remarks

The novel may boast of the absence of the powerful white faction, yet a close and detailed study reveals that they are present, and their presence is felt both by the powerful and the powerless individuals of the African American community at large, leading to a notion of confined space. Harlem becomes a representative space where, in spite of the apparent fragmentation, all the Blacks feel a sense of community, inherently derived from their respective cultures, practices and belief systems. It is a space with no clear hierarchy or cultural winner, where elements from both the Orient and the Occident play their part in the crime and its detection. While the crime of the initial murder of Frimbo's servant N'Ogo is due to the combination of Oriental law dictating the importance of tribal chiefs and Frimbo's Occidental knowledge by which he devises the mathematical formulation for winning money, so does the detection part involve both Oriental and Occident elements. It is the combination of Oriental dictums of kingship, which makes the tribal chief Frimbo lose his own life to detect the murderer of his servant, and Occidental, scientific study of the crime and the clues, which varies from fingerprint to dental bridges. Therefore, it is safe to conclude that, in Fisher's *The Conjure Man Dies: A Mystery Tale of Dark Harlem*, Harlem symbolizes a space where under the rubric of dissimilation, there is an assimilation of cultures. On the surface level it may appear that the two communities are disunited on the grounds of social and cultural practices. While the Occidentals do not consider their African heritage of any importance and seem to have adapted themselves to their Western identities and have accepted Western rationalism as part of their code of conduct, the Orientals uphold and take pride in their African cultural heritage and are much more compassionate towards preserving their cultural practices by making them a part of their lived experience. Despite this stark difference, a detailed study of the text reveals that it is a space where the powerful confluence of two cultures takes place.

WORKS CITED

Ashcroft, Bill, et al., editors. *Post-Colonial Studies: The Key Concepts.* 2nd ed., Routledge, 2007.

Bailey, Frankie Y. *Out of the Woodpile: Black Characters in Crime and Detective Fiction.* Greenwood, 1991.

Balshaw, Maria. *Looking for Harlem: Urban Aesthetics in African American Literature.* Pluto Press, 2000.

Bell, Bernard. *The Afro-American Novel and Its Tradition.* Massachusetts UP, 1987.

Brown, Lois. *Encyclopedia of the Harlem Literary Renaissance.* Facts on File, 2006.

Condé, Mary. "The 'almost bitter murmur' in Rudolph Fisher's *The Conjure Man Dies.*" *"Polar noir": Reading African-American Detective Fiction.* Edited by Mills, Alice, and Claude Julien, Presses universitaires François-Rabelais, 2005, pp. 13-21. books.openedition.org/pufr/5776.

Corbould, Clare. *Becoming African Americans: Black Public Life in Harlem, 1919–1939.* Harvard UP, 2009.

Deutsch, Leonard J. "Rudolph Fisher's Unpublished Manuscripts: Description and Commentary." *Obsidian* (1975-1982), vol. 6, no. 1/2, 1980, pp. 82–97. JSTOR, jstor.org/stable/44489757.

Fisher, Rudolph. *The Conjure Man Dies: A Mystery Tale of Dark Harlem*. 1932. Michigan UP, 1992.

Francaviglia, Richard V. *Go East, Young Man: Imagining the American West as the Orient*. U of Utah P, 2011.

Gandhi, Leela. "Preface." *Postcolonial Theory: A Critical Introduction*. Columbia UP, 1998, pp. viii-x.

Gosselin, Adrienne Johnson. "The World Would Do Better to Ask Why Is Frimbo Sherlock Holmes?: Investigating Liminality in Rudolph Fisher's *The Conjure-Man Dies*." *African American Review*, vol. 32, no. 4, 1998, pp. 607–619. JSTOR, jstor.org/stable/2901240.

Green, Dan S., and Edwin D. Driver, editors. *W.E.B. Du Bois on Sociology and the Black Community*. Chicago UP, 1978.

James, P.D. *Talking about Detective Fiction*. Knopf, 2009.

Mirmotahari, Emad. "Harlemite, Detective, African? The Many Selves of Rudolph Fisher's *Conjure-Man Dies*." *Callaloo*, vol. 36, no. 2, 2013, pp. 268–278. JSTOR, jstor.org/stable/24264908.

Neely, Barbara. *Blanche Among the Talented Tenth*. Kindle ed., Brash books, 2014.

Peterson, Carla L. "What Renaissance?: A Deep Genealogy of Black Culture in Nineteenth-Century New York City." *A Companion to the Harlem Renaissance*. Edited by Cherene Sherrard-Johnson, Wiley Blackwell, 2015, pp. 17-34.

Poupard, Dennis, editor. *Twentieth-Century Literary Criticism*. vol. 11, Gale Research, 1983.

Priestman, Martin. *Crime Fiction: From Poe to the Present*. Northcote House, 1998.

Scruggs, Charles. "Sexual Desire, Modernity, and Modernism in the Fiction of Nella Larsen and Rudolph Fisher." *The Cambridge Companion to the Harlem Renaissance*. Edited by George Hutchinson, Cambridge UP, 2007, pp. 155-169.

Soitos, Stephen F. *The Blues Detective: A Study of African-American Detective Fiction.* U of Massachusetts P, 1996.

Southgate, Robert L. *Black Plots & Black Characters: A Handbook for Afro-American Literature.* Gaylord Professional Publications, 1979.

Taylor, Monique M. *Harlem between Heaven and Hell.* U of Minnesota P, 2002.

Todorov, Tzvetan. *The Poetics of Prose.* Translated by Richard Howard, Cornell UP, 1977.

Watson, Rachel. "Blood Typing: Rudolph Fisher's *The Conjure-Man Dies.*" *CLA Journal*, vol. 61, no. 4, 2018, pp. 165–184. JSTOR, jstor.org/stable/10.34042/claj.61.4.0165.

Wintz, Cary D., and Paul Finkelman, editors. *Encyclopedia of the Harlem Renaissance*, vol. 1, Routledge, 2004.

Woods, Paula L., editor. *Spooks, Spies, and Private Eyes: Black Mystery, Crime, and Suspense Fiction.* Doubleday, 1995.

Institutional Paradox in the City: Duality, Domiciles, and Death in Dickens's London

Meghan P. Nolan

Abstract

The city has long been the perfect backdrop for detective fiction, as its contradictory qualities breed mysterious circumstances— a paradox that is particularly perceptible in relation to key features of urban geography which were formed by social institutions. Interestingly, many of the neighborhood and district delimitations within the world's largest metropolitan areas today can be directly traced to institutional developments in the mid-nineteenth century. And while New York is one of the best conurbations to analyze in this context, London too was solidifying its social geography as one of the most rapidly expanding metropolises of the Victorian era both publicly and financially.

Because no other novel covers the breadth and depth of New York's European counterpart quite like Charles Dickens's *Bleak House*, this essay contends that the failures of London's social institutions can be seen through the deaths of two corresponding characters in the novel. More specifically, this essay analyzes how Dickens uses descriptions of the domiciles and the death scenes of four specific twosomes to highlight social disorder within the systems of justice, commerce, welfare, and social hierarchy respectively and reveal stark contradictions within these heavily ingrained (and often cherished) constructs of urban society.

Introduction

The city has long been the perfect backdrop for detective fiction, primarily because its contradictory qualities breed mysterious circumstances, particularly through an inescapable insistence upon socioeconomic separation and defined borders that is defied by a locality which does not in fact allow for such clear distinctions. However, these types of boundaries persist because, as many social and geographical analysts argue, the "key features of urban morphology and social geography were produced by characteristic social institutions and practices" (Glennie 927).[1] Interestingly, many of the neighborhood and district delimitations within the world's largest metropolitan areas today can be directly traced to institutional developments in the mid-nineteenth century. For instance, in the 1850s commerce helped to shape many of New York City's most recognizable neighborhoods: Although "The area between City Hall and Twenty-third street was the most densely populated [at the time], … below City Hall was devoted almost exclusively to Trade," Broadway became the center of commerce, and Fifth, Madison, and Lexington streets were newly designated the most fashionable areas for the City's elite (Epstein 29). London, England, was concurrently expanding and demarcating in much the same way, and no other novel covers the breadth and depth of New York's European counterpart quite like Charles Dickens's *Bleak House*.

"London" (Dickens 17). This singular beginning to *Bleak House* fixes the framework for the rest of the novel and the tremendous magnitude of its overarching goal— its complete dedication to exposing the vast dimensions of the City as an expression of its totality: "As with all great cities, the dichotomous nature of Victorian London easily lends itself to the mystery genre, because it is simultaneously vast and condensed in landscape, diverging construction, ideals and people abut and overlap within its many warrens" (Nolan 135). Originally serialized between 1852 - 1853, the narrative acts very much like an historical map of London's many intersections, topographical and social, through its layering of characters—including "the first 'detective hero' in British fiction," Inspector Bucket (Ben-Merre

50)—authentic location descriptions, and circumstances surrounding several concurrent mysteries. And so there is no more important
factor than the metropolis itself in this novel, as London is central to
the understanding of the complex narrative in ingenious ways, and
its portrayal is the reason that *Bleak House* is so often considered one
of Dickens's best works. Truly, from that single word of commence-
ment, Dickens's profound fascination with the immense extremes of
the City begins to form the contours of an expansive urban environment. And, upon close inspection, intricate patterns of connectivity
begin to emerge within the myriad limits of this densely populated
conurbation.

    Bleak House uniquely focuses on a barrage of secondary charac-
ters in an effort to paint an accurate picture of the City's distinctive
denizens. And, in true Dickensian fashion, even the omniscient
narrator of *Bleak House* muses about the possible connections among
the novel's seemingly infinite population: "What connexion can there
have been between many people in the innumerable histories of this
world..." (220). Outwardly, the linkage is derived from the need for a
unified ending— the concept that the characters and their associative
plot arcs and mysteries intentionally overlap with each other as the
story progresses in order to draw some logical conclusion. However,
if these characters are viewed as dimensions of the larger precept of
London, then their relations extend far beyond this basic ideal, as
they begin to symbolize the various strata of the City's inherently
transformative existence. And so, the famed initial declaration of
Bleak House also sets the stage for viewing London from multiple
perspectives.

    Murray Baumgarten's reference to Dickens's London as "a living
cityscape" (219) perpetuates the idea of the City as an animate organ-
ism. Accordingly, if London is viewed as a character in *Bleak House*,
then it is certainly the most complex and well-developed character;
the only one, it is worth noting, around which every mystery hinges,
a claim that not even the novel's detective can make. And the City,
like any sophisticated protagonist, has countless façades which are
ripe with flaws— suitably, its many facets are expressed as the very
institutions that are designed to hold it together. Certainly, in a city

as large as London, social institutions play a large role in connecting and defining its exacting boundaries. And so, it is only natural that the establishment of such communal ideals would grow in complexity as the conurbation and its diverse set of inhabitants expand. In London, as in all major metropolises, social order extends beyond religious edicts, and public conventions like the law are thought of as keeping order for the benefit the people at large.

Scholars like Caroline Levine argue that these globalized institutions are represented by a series of connective networks that tie together seemingly disparate storylines (and their respective mysteries). Specifically, she states that *Bleak House* structures the unfolding of its plot(s) around these multiple conflicting and competing webs of interconnection, and thus the narrative is developed explicitly around communal hubs of politics, economics, and technology (519).[2] Seemingly, Dickens's London is also a place of pure satire where these formal institutions fail time and time again, and so Emily Steinlight amusingly refers to these networks as a "series of experiments in population management" (229), because of their repeated inability to provide for the masses in the ways they claim:

> In *Bleak House*, where politics is a sham and where "telescopic philanthropy" (49), local pastorship, and familial relations alike prove more destructive than beneficial, all professions of humanitarian sympathy and instances of direct intervention only set into stark relief the seemingly inevitable failure of any individual or institution either to "provide for" or to "dispose of" an apparent surplus of human life. (229)

Steinlight's grouping of the individual and the institution is important in that it highlights the fact that a singular character cannot be easily separated from any construct of which he/she is a part. Therefore, her declaration that *Bleak House*'s social ideals continuously fail to provide valid services for the greater good is directly echoed in the novel through Dickens's depictions of various characters. And, while social networks and their eminent failures become obvious throughout the novel at length, there is greater value to each individual character beyond his/her inclusion in any number of these socially defined networks—this includes those characters who would typically be considered as purely secondary, as they often possess evidence or knowledge necessary to solve a given mystery. As it is a common understanding that Dickens's characters act as gross exaggerations of the social stereotypes found in the metropolis at the time, it is also possible for each character (as opposed to the connective networks themselves) to signify amplifications of these major social institutions. Therefore, a particular social institution may be directly represented by multiple characters throughout the novel as a way of demonstrating the complexities within each façade. And, in turn, the faults of such institutions can be found in the development, domicile, and demise of each appointed character throughout the novel.

This concept is further amplified as Dickens often uses forms of extended parataxis to juxtapose a given institution's veneer with what he deems its more unpleasant reality via the very space that represents it within the City, and it is in this complex identification schema that a sense of collective anxiety begins to materialize. Baumgarten asserts that Dickens's London is invariably crowded with these discrete contradictions and their impending disquietude:

> These contradictory feelings often accompany the cognitive dissonance of the urban scene, which becomes both the condition for the experience and expression of its multiplicities. Dickens moves the reader through events—psychic, political, social, [and] communal. (219)

Hence, Baumgarten proclaims that the resonating tension of the novel is created by the compound association of complex paradoxes within the novel's social paradigms. The noticeable uneasiness that he refers to as "cognitive dissonance" is not just the result of these urban tropes colliding as Dickens navigates the City, but it is also the product of an intense uncertainty surrounding these supposedly well-established institutions. Undoubtedly, this effect is heightened as Dickens epitomizes concrete and essential metropolitan ideals via their assigned characters and locations, and then eventually discloses the inimitable truths of these social foundations through those characters' deaths. As a result, the pervasive imbalance becomes so prominent that even the characters within the novel comment on its strangeness— the perpetually confused Law-Stationer, Mr. Snagsby, perceptively notes to himself that "[s]omething is wrong, some-where" (344) in a direct parody of the deeper disquiet that surrounds London's disparate factions.

Therefore, this essay contends that the representational façades of the character of London are approached through the deaths of two corresponding characters. More specifically, Dickens uses descriptions of domiciles and the death scenes of these characters to reveal stark contradictions within these heavily ingrained (and often cherished) constructs of urban society. This intention becomes particularly perceptible through the careful examination of what remains after a given paradigm has perished. And, although there are many such character pairings throughout the novel, four specific twosomes speak directly to social disorder within the systems of justice, commerce, welfare, and social hierarchy respectively.

The Injured and the Usurper – The Heart of the City

Dickens is enthralled with what Jeremy Bentham, a renowned philosopher and social reformer of the time, calls "fictions of the law" that are deliberately designed "to serve the sinister interests of lawyers, judges, and all those who profit from legal procedures, rather than the happiness of the 'greatest number'" (Stone 130).[3] In reference to Steinlight's remarks on institutional failure, *Bleak House* pivots around the court case of Jarndyce v. Jarndyce famously known therein for its infinite illusiveness and preposterous timeframe. Of this judicial folly, Dickens writes, "… everything set forth in these pages concerning the Court of Chancery is substantially true, and within the truth" (5). And so, he strikes a timely blow in support of the Chancery Procedure Act of 1852, according to Marjorie Stone, as many of these fictions and forms were abolished thereafter (141). Dickens's intentional use of a lawsuit as a satirical backdrop for the City's perplexing legal system and its resultant mysteries gives a profound weight to the institution's faults, as the injured and the usurper are presented as two equal weights upon the scales of justice. Subsequently, Dickens uses authentic portrayals of the legal system to demonstrate the difference between the Law and its powerless victims, and this is best expressed through needless deaths.

Dieter Paul Polloczek argues that differentiated contradictions and expectations begin to coexist in Dickens's London because of the legal system's infiltration of the private sector. This can be seen not only in the figurative sense, but in the physical sense as well, as several characters reside in regrettable proximity to the law offices of Chancery— "Chancery [where all of the novel's legal machinations occur] is located in the heart of the City of London. It includes the Courts [Inns of Courts, and law firms], where lawsuits grind their way slowly through bureaucratic motions and remotions" (Hale "In Chancery"). Moreover, this indecisiveness of the law often results in the sometimes contradictory way that characters readjust and perpetuate their own lives (Polloczek 465). And, although there are many throughout the novel who are required to adapt to in order to accommodate the Jarndyce case, the Chancery suit of Mr. Gridley is far more potent for exposing the degradation that occurs at the hand of misguided legal tactics. Known as "The man from Shropshire" (13), Mr. Gridley has a connection to the formal institution that is far more significant because his story is based in actual history. Dickens claims that "[t]he case of Gridley is in no essential altered from one of actual occurrence, made public by a disinterested person who was professionally acquainted with the whole of the monstrous wrong from beginning to end" (5). His insistence on the very realness of the victimization of Gridley further speaks to his beliefs regarding the injustice surrounding the chancery process.

Essentially, Gridley is forced upon the law as a means of trying to claim his rightful inheritance after the death of his parents. Although the will itself is not contested, a question arises about whether a portion of the inheritance has already been paid and turns what should be a simple court case into a lengthy ordeal during which Gridley's birthright is questioned and the whole estate goes directly to the court in order to pay for mounting legal costs. Sadly, even though

Gridley attempts to adjust to his unfortunate situation, the repeated failure of his bargaining attempts eventually embitters him, and he becomes so altered by his circumstance that it is said that "[h]is countenance had, perhaps for years, become so set in its contentious expression that it did not soften even … when he was quiet" (217)—a grim disposition mimicked by his equally grim living situation as a tenant of Mrs. Blinder's in a narrow alley in Bell Yard among various publishers, tradesmen, and orphaned children (210).

Gridley (whose name literally suggests that he is "gridlocked" as a result of the legal system) is an undeniable example of the victim of justice. Even from a personal vantage point, he is able to recognize that the very system that is supposed to protect his interests has in fact taken them away. As a result of this insight, he is atypically allowed to openly criticize the institutional system he represents:

> "There again!" said Mr. Gridley, with no diminution of his rage. "The system! I am told, on all hands, it's the system. I mustn't look to individuals. It's the system. … Have you the face to tell me I have received justice, and therefore am dismissed? … I don't know what may happen if I am carried beyond myself at last! — I will accuse the individual workers of that system against me, face to face, before the great eternal bar!" (216 – 217)

Gridley asserts that individuals cannot be separated from the faulty institution, and he therefore holds them equally responsible. And, as prophesized, this insatiable hate extends until his dying day, when he unnecessarily passes away in Mr. George's shooting gallery, which is so unfortunately located in "that curious region lying about the Haymarket and Leicester Square which is a centre of attraction to indifferent foreign hotels and indifferent foreigners, racket-courts, fighting-men, swordsmen, footguards, old china, gaming-houses, exhibitions, and a large medley of shabbiness and shrinking out of sight" (299) as opposed to his bequeathed property, which has been pilfered from him by the justice system. Insult is added to injury when he is hunted down and harassed upon his death bed by Inspector Bucket, who is an extension of the legal system as a representative of law enforcement. In the end, Gridley is depicted as the pitifully wounded, and although he is decidedly irascible in life (in accordance with Polloczek's alteration theory), he continues to be posthumously sentimentalized as the Victim through the words of characters like Mr. George and Ms. Flite.

The antithesis of judicial suffering is expressed as the outright intimidation by those very practitioners of the system whom Gridley lays blame upon. Lawyers like Conversation Kenge may talk a big game, but out of all of the barristers in *Bleak House*, Tulkinghorn is by far the most incredible in his role as usurper. Undeniably, he is the precise exemplification of Bentham's predatory lawman (Stone 130) as he forever seeks control over others. He is centralized both in physical location and involvement. As a result, he is described as being "[a]lways at hand. Haunting every place. No relief or security from him for a moment" (613). Tulkinghorn's placement affords him the ability to further entrench himself in the most important mysteries, as he meets with Lady Dedlock, the Smallweeds, and Hortence independently in order to gather information within his lavish chambers in the City's center at Lincoln's Inn Fields. And so, like the justice system itself, he is established as the one holding all the proverbial cards. Consequently, rather than acting in earnest, this knower of secrets becomes the puppeteer perpetually pulling the strings on his associates. Tulkinghorn shows the true extent of this power during a final discussion with Lady Dedlock in light of her possible exposure as a counterfeit and fallen woman, for it is at that time that he orders her to remain at Chesney Wold until he gives further notice (549). And, while Chesney Wold may not be the worst place to be held captive— "located in Lincolnshire, some distance to the North of London. As an Estate, Chesney Wold has many buildings, including the main house itself, a church or chapel, parkland, and farmland" (Hale "In Chesney Wold") — this arrangement deliberately places Tulkinghorn in complete power over the situation, and also over Lady Dedlock's interests and whereabouts for better or worse.

However, it is not until this solicitor's mysterious (but hardly unexpected) murder in his own aforementioned chambers that Dickens alludes to the real issue of the usurper of legal affairs. It is fitting that the representative of justice, who is always in control, meets his death at the hands of an equally cunning character. Although the means of his demise appear to be unjust, the law still prevails, as the de facto courier, Bucket, hunts and captures Hortence as Tulkinghorn's murderer. More importantly, however, his death reveals the all-encompassing reach of the justice system across the City and beyond, as even after his death, his initial assertion that the Dedlock marriage bond should be broken is carried out through Lady Dedlock's pervasive decline. And so, it turns out that his physical presence is not needed for the control of the justice system to be maintained. Tulkinghorn is but a pawn for the institution that reigns regardless of expendable bodies, thus rendering him unnecessary.

And so, even though Gridley directly indicts individuals like Tulkinghorn for his personal misfortune, in the end Dickens proclaims that the system, which is concentrated in the center of the City and permeates every crevice, is still ultimately responsible for the gross injustices of the law. Thus, his contradiction of the justice system is accomplished through his exemplification of legal regulators and the impending doom of their intended prey, and the same could be said of those who conduct other types of business within this City as well.

The Consumer and the Investor – The Business District

Undoubtedly, commercial industry is crucial to the subsistence of any major city, and as previously mentioned, London, like New York, was one of the most rapidly expanding metropolises of the Victorian era both publicly and financially. Subsequently, various forms of business permeate all of Dickens's novels, according to Stone, in a way that makes it utterly inseparable from the more domestic sphere of his works (143). And thus, official business or commerce is an urban necessity that must be comprehensively detailed within *Bleak House*.

As a city devoted to business, and frequently to the discrete and complex business of the Law, Dickens's London is adroitly populated with capitalists who practice their trade to various degrees. Most importantly, it seems that for every legitimate businessman in this cityscape there are two illegitimate counterparts. The aforementioned Stationer, Mr. Snagsby, plies his trade rightfully, and therefore his business practices are never put into question as the narrative advances. His location in Cook's Court (based on the real Took's Court) Cursitor Street near Chancery is also respectable, efficient, and central to all storylines. Contrastingly, however, characters such as the Smallweeds tend to represent a faction of formidable loan sharks who permeate the City with more dubious intentions, and so Dickens purposefully locates them "[i]n a rather ill-favoured and ill-savoured neighbourhood ... [on] a little narrow street, always solitary, shady, and sad, closely bricked on all sides like a tomb" and illustrates several of their malicious acts "in the dark little parlour certain feet below the level of the street" (284 - 285).

Through his underhanded dealings with Mr. George, Mr. Smallweed (the uncontested ring-leader of detestable financiers) represents the public institution of banking and its critical failure to provide an unfettered product.[4] And so, Dickens is able to frequently tackle hidden corruptions in the commerce system through the detailed undertakings of such characters. But public banking is only one aspect of the larger issues of commerce, as the heart of any business endeavor rests strictly upon supply and demand. Hence, the consumer and the investor are the two crucial sides of the commercial coin, and Dickens's warning about this institution is twofold through his depiction of general business practices in *Bleak House*. Specifically, caveats are most evident in the byproducts of those deaths which consist of unusual forms of annihilation.

There is only one businessman in *Bleak House* who appears *not* to conduct any business at all— Krook, the proprietor of "Krook, Rag and Bottle Warehouse" leads a curious existence, for "[e]verything seemed to be bought, and nothing sold" (63). Krook is mysteriously and independently wealthy, as the genesis of his property ownership is unknown, but his shop's placement neighboring Chancery epitomizes his entanglement in several of the novel's central mysteries, including Nemo's identification, Esther's parentage, and the Jarndyce and Jarndyce case. And, although connections can be directly drawn to his associations with the Smallweeds, it is clear that his relationship is familial rather than financial. Because of his independent wealth and the income from lodgers, Krook is able to spend the majority of his time "collecting" items rather than hawking them. This holds special significance when considering Krook's obvious connection to the primary business of the novel, as he obtains items mainly pertaining specifically to the law in one fashion or another. And so this immeasurable propensity for accumulation establishes Krook as the ideal consumer in business, and his constant hoarding becomes a direct reference to extreme forms of acquisition consistent with urban consumerism then and now.

Krook's death is one of the most provocative and bizarre of all, as the narrator proclaims that he perishes as the result of "[s]pontaneous Combustion, and none other of all the deaths that can be died" (Dickens 436). Brooke D. Taylor posits that the inclusion of this strange method of casualty is meant to explore "the tension between what we intuitively feel and what we can empirically prove" (173). In this context, Krook's spontaneous combustion becomes a commentary on the detriments of flagrant consumerism within the vast metropolis; the reader feels it is inappropriate but can find no definitive proof of it. And, beyond Dickens's insistence in the preface that combustion is a real form of death (6), the necessity for a fatal outburst can be found in examining its after-effects. For, in this controversial and much debated death scene, little is left of Krook in the end but his essence:

> Here is a small burnt paper, but not so light as usual,
> seeming to be steeped in something; and here is— is it
> the cinder of a small charred and broken log of wood
> sprinkled with white ashes, or is it coal? O Horror, he
> IS here! and this ... is all that represents him. (436)

The narrator asserts that because of the quick outward incineration, all that remains of this character are the byproducts of his former self. This is appropriate commentary for a representative of the commercial domain, as it appears that Krook has literally consumed until he can consume no more. And so, the act of combustion is the outward explosion of all that he has taken in. In addition, Krook physically leaves behind a residue after death in the form of a "black fat" (430), an odorous "yellow liquor" (433), and an inventory of eccentric wares, which have no true resale value in the public-sphere. These combined deposits represent the lingering surplus of mass consumer consumption. As Krook's existence can no longer support the detritus of the system, he becomes a cautionary tale to a rapidly expanding middle class of the dangers of such intake, and thus it is the first warning of excessive practices in commerce.

Conversely, Richard Carstone's bullish approach to all of his business affairs, including the Jarndyce suit, solidifies him as the representative of the incessant investor. Richard's position as an archetype of London's most risky investors is at first defined through his distinct refusal to earn an income through traditional means of employment and his change of locations— after a series of bad speculation, he moves from the more desirable, upper-class suburbs to several intermediary locations like the army barracks, and eventually lands in "a dull room, fadedly furnished" (647) conveniently next door to the office of his exploiter, Mr. Vholes, in Symond's Inn, which itself is said to be perpetually in the dark because it is "squeezed up in a corner and blinks at a dead wall" (517). As the venture capitalist denounces more conventional speculations, Richard walks away from several well-respected vocations in order to capitalize on a decidedly uncertain proposition in the form of his expected inheritance from the law suit. Furthermore, the fundamental key to understanding Richard's role as the investor is found in a resounding catch phrase: As the story progresses he repeatedly exclaims, "I will begin the world!" (Ch. 65) in opposition to what is seen as his imminent decline. Beaumont explains that, "In the nineteenth century, 'to begin the world' was a common colloquial expression for commencing a life of financial independence" (808). And so, it appears that Richard's expostulation and the concordant title to the chapter of his death directly reference his need for financial freedom stemming from his initial designation as a ward. As a result of this persistent angling for independent wealth, Richard constantly makes perilous business decisions and invests money and energy in all the wrong places as he perpetually seeks to further his role as a prominent investor, rather than laborer. Unfortunately, there is a limit to Richard's unremitting output.

Richard's passing is comparable to Krook's in its unusualness, as he comes to an end in an equally dramatic (although less controversial) form of annihilation. But, that's where the similarities cease, as it appears that the sheer quantity of Richard's ventures catch up with him— consuming him to the core. As the consummate investor, Richard begins to contribute health and heart when his monetary means of investment run dry. At this point, Esther remarks in her narrative that he takes on the "darkened look" of those who have been devoured by similar endeavors (497). Rightfully, this marks the beginning of the end for Richard, and at the exact moment of his death, the narrator circulates back to the pitiable phrase: "and with one parting sob [he] began the world" (808). This reference indicates the importance that the risk of financial independence plays in Richard's ultimate demise. And so, *his* is a protracted internal death that counters that of Krook, as he in effect dwindles slowly into nothingness—losing everything but his unborn child in the process.

Both of these inexplicable forms of death result in a yawning gap in the system of commerce, as either form leads to an uncertain and regrettable outcome as a result of an overindulgence that is so common in such business epicenters. Thus, Dickens concludes his interrogation of the inconsistencies of commerce as he demonstrates the absolute obliteration that is the result of economic depletion in its various forms, but he also makes it clear that this kind of dysfunction spreads past the city's perimeter as well.

The Indigent and the Indolent – The Suburbs

Throughout the nineteenth century, social reform was at the forefront of literary concern, and by way of the factual reports of Friedrich Engels and various social-problem novels, such as Elizabeth Gaskell's *Mary Barton*, the plight of the urban poor began to form the underpinnings of the era's ethical debates. Additionally, Carmen Mangion claims that these written documentations were supported in real life by movements of Catholic and Protestant reformers who were working toward the betterment of some of the described conditions through the establishment of community-managed alternatives to disgracefully commonplace conventions like poor law workhouses (515). And so, although public assistance for the poor was far from the types of governmental systems that exist today, a greater sense of consciousness was beginning to take form, and the result was a heightened mainstream awareness of a public responsibility for the poor as a system of generalized social welfare. Correspondingly, *Bleak House* echoes these concerns, and the advent of a welfare system is clearly identified through several of the novel's recurring characters not only inside city limits (e.g., Jo, the street sweeper of Tom-All-Alone's), but in the suburbs as well.

Bleak House is one of the few texts of its time to address the more undesirable sentiment surrounding established public aid. Indeed, Dickens spends a considerable amount of time chastising misguided attempts at philanthropy via characters like Mrs. Jellyby, Mr. Quale, and Mrs. Pardiggle. Nevertheless, Dickens makes it clear that the indigent and the indolent are two tines on the same philanthropic fork, and he presents these twin issues of welfare in order to unearth the immense incongruities that exist as a result of such formalized charity. Interestingly, this dichotomy is most noticeable through often ignored scenes of "infant" mortality in the outskirts of town, an indication of how the institution's shortcomings cannot help but to bleed beyond municipal borders.

Although *Bleak House* is concentrated in London (as opposed to its more industrial little sister, Manchester), the working class is still plainly embodied as a part of its populace even in its suburbs. Mainly, this representation is achieved through individuals like the brick-makers and their wives (one of whom, Jenny, becomes directly involved in the mystery of the protagonist, Esther's parentage). And so, the necessity for a common welfare system is demonstrated through the description of their calamitous living conditions. They (the indigent) are described as living in complete squalor, as their dwelling near Bleak House in the northern outskirts of London in St. Albans is depicted as "one of a cluster of wretched hovels in a brick-field, with pigsties close to broken windows, and miserable

little gardens before the doors, growing nothing but stagnant pools"
(114). This account is meant to prove that these laborers exist in
various states of desperation as a result of poor living and working
conditions. Theirs is a common story of hard work with little reward,
filled with bitter disappointment, and a perpetual cycle of physical
and emotional abuse. But the veritable tragedy of their lives is only
completely revealed as the baby of one of the brick-makers passes
away— for, it is at that point that Dickens uncovers an undeniable
justification for a welfare system. As the perished infant lies on its
mother's lap, Ada (an agent of the system of inheritance) echoes public sentiment when she says, "'This suffering, quiet, pretty little thing!
I am so sorry for it. I am so sorry for the mother. I never saw a sight
so pitiful as this before'" (118). Later, this response is compounded as
Jenny, the mother of the unfortunate child, proclaims that he is better
off dead (and incidentally luckier than the rest), because the mere act
of survival is too painful to wish upon another. The sheer thought
of a newborn dying in such a manner tugs at the proverbial heart
strings, and thus gives credence to the need for a genuinely charitable
system in society. This scene and its subsequent aftermath expose the
positive desire to contribute to the well-being of the indigent in order
to avoid a parallel prospect, as few can impugn an infant for being
born into such conditions. However, unlike other authors of the day,
Dickens is not wholly sentimental, and so he also presents this construct's evil alter ego.

In *Bleak House*, the converse of underprivileged necessity comes
in the form of gross consumption of charity by those who are undeserving. Harold Skimpole, also an "infant" (although self-pro-
claimed), is the quintessential social parasite who, in complete
opposition to the brick-makers, manages to survive without working
a single day in his life. In essence, he bilks the system by illegitimately
proclaiming his infancy, and thus reaping the rewards of an intended
welfare system in the form of such basic amenities as food, shelter,
and money, a fact that is exemplified by his transient inhabitation
of the homes of the wealthy (namely, that of John Jarndyce at Bleak
House), despite the fact that he has a home of his own where his wife
and children reside. What is more, he persists this way for almost the

entirety of the novel bouncing from one institutional representative to the next, and all the time crafting new ways to incur said benefits. As irksome as Skimpole's existence is, Dickens reserves the ultimate consequence of this kink in the welfare system until Skimpole's uneventful death (which is intentionally alluded to only briefly in Esther's narrative toward the conclusion of the novel). Pure irony abounds, as this tiresome free-loader manages to earn money posthumously through the publication of his slanderous autobiography, in which he defames those who aided him most (773), and thus makes a mockery of the entire system. Indeed, Skimpole's character is indicative of the indolent, as he is a constant drain on society throughout his lifetime and even continues to defy genuine necessity long after he is gone.

And so Dickens's paradox of the welfare system is complete as the undeserving hanger-on continues to profit after death, while those who desperately require aid endlessly endure poverty and destitution. The juxtaposition of the two locations, the brick yard and Bleak House, both on the outskirts of London, also serve to represent the pervasiveness of such dysfunction. Thus, the simultaneous representation of these two factors expresses the combined demand for contribution to and caution of a welfare system that can often lead one to an early grave despite best intentions.

The Anonymous and the Infamous – The Pauper's Cemetery

Even with an emergent middle class, social hierarchy was deeply entrenched in Victorian cities, because "while socioeconomic borders and hierarchal standards abound in this environment, the upper and lower classes remain intertwined and mutually dependent" whether they acknowledge it or not (Nolan 135). This division is often painfully evident in 1850s New York, where areas like Five Points (overpopulated and rife with disease and destitution) are adjacent to the City's financial district (Epstein 31), and it is equally as prevalent in London, where "Tom-All-Alone's, a London slum, is within walking distance of the bureaucratic muddle, whirl, and inaction of Chancery" (Hale "Tom-All-Alone's"). Class divides were often expressed as insurmountable gaps, and authors like Benjamin Disraeli addressed matters of social mobility only peripherally in literary works. While *Bleak House* does not directly seek to make any of its characters upwardly mobile, it does seem to question the ideals of inherent birthright. Dickens examines class identifications and shifting capacities of inheritance through several characters throughout the narrative, namely the many wards of Jarndyce. Yet, he is clear about the distinctions between these classes, especially as no character actually transcends beyond his/her proper place within the hierarchal chain or corresponding locations. Certainly, the limitations of these ideals create constraints for those characters who hover in between, and Polloczek believes that "… while these characters implicitly consent to principles of subjection, subjectivation, and civil society, they are either treated as, or feel like, someone guilty of turning against those principles" (465). So, because the anonymous and the infamous are two jewels on the same scepter of social hierarchy, Dickens seeks to expose this irony through those death scenes that are linked to the pauper's cemetery.

Although little of Captain Hawdon's story can be discerned (in fact, he is one of the few characters not fully developed in the novel and thus remains a mystery to a great extent), he becomes an important factor in the understanding of the incongruous nature of the hierarchal system. Undoubtedly, he marks his designation as the anonymous when he chooses to go by the name Nemo, or "No-man," in a clear effort to be forgotten and lost among the throngs of the City. And because his birthright is unknown, he initially supersedes the need for a prescribed social status. In Dickens's London, however, the connective networks and institutional bonds are so intimately joined that it is nearly impossible for an individual to remain entirely anonymous.

Therefore, Nemo's death exposes an interesting flaw of social hierarchy. Nemo's passing takes the form of self-imposed degeneration, as he chooses to deliberately overdose on opium in a sparsely furnished flat located above Krook's shop. After his death, the interest of others is perpetuated by the need to classify him. That is to say, yet another mystery ensues as characters desperately try to identify the anonymous in order to assign an appropriate social rank—they need to decide his rightful place. However, Kemper Columbus states that "Nemo's corpse, described as 'deserted infant,' indicates how not only his childhood, not only his history, but his entire life has been eclipsed" (615 – 616). So this too is ironic in the sense that although Nemo manages to be overlooked more than once in life, it is impossible for him to continue this in death because of the fundamental need for social identification.

Conversely, Lady Dedlock appears to be emblematic of all things aristocratic. Her Christian name, Honoria, implies that she is of high moral standing, and her proud manner distinguishes her as "… an inscrutable Being, quite out of reach and ken of ordinary mortals" (27). In fact, several characters of various classes recognize her by this hallmark throughout the narrative, and she maintains her patrician bearing even when disguised as a servant. However, tightly condensed paradoxes develop as Lady Dedlock's roots cannot be legitimately traced in blue-blood, and so her venerated grace turns out to be an affected one. In this sense, she becomes a direct mockery of aristocratic form and function, because in Dickens's estimation, it is nothing more than a practiced air. (Incidentally, this farce is articulated through Mr. Turveydrop's performed "deportment" as well.) This juxtaposition of qualities in Lady Dedlock's existence is fundamentally ironic because she manages to deliberately evade detection among the very aristocrats who place such high value on birthright. She is also doubly infamous, then: at first for her upper-class façade and finally for her sordid past.

And so, Lady Dedlock sees death as the only way out of her circumstance, thus demonstrating the greatest contradiction of the system of social hierarchy. Her years of play-acting constrict her in unexpected ways, and so she desperately seeks to revert back to the illegitimacy from which she came. Polloczek states that she needs "… to escape into a literal death, which thus becomes the focus of an escape from that very metaphorical death which imprisoned her life in isolation" (467). This intentional fall of hierarchal ideals marks the beginning of her physical and mental degeneration. Her grueling journey from the fashionable suburbs of Lincolnshire to the brick maker's shack to the filthy streets of London on foot is emblematic of her fall from grace—it capitulates in death and her cold dead body lies upon the filthy stoop of a cemetery for the underprivileged where she is mistaken for the indigent (Jenny) by her own daughter (Dickens 756). This "unnatural death" signifies the retreat of pomp and circumstance, as she loses her aristocratic luster and reassumes the demeanor of a mere mortal.

Subsequently, Dickens's final paradox is complete as the dual factors of social hierarchy, Captain Hawdon/ Nemo and Lady Dedlock, deteriorate into remnants of their former selves, only to end up at the exact same pauper's grave despite the drastically different circumstances and locations that led them there. Additional satire can be found in the stark contrast of the public figure who wishes to be forgotten versus the private individual who is forced into exposure as the result of death. And yet, Hortence's words are a constant reminder that regardless of class, "'It is but death, it is all the same'" (694).

Conclusion

In *Bleak House*, inherent paradoxes of social institutions play a major role in the development of the greater character of London, as all of these contradictory facets exist seamlessly within the transformative body of the City. Truly, things are not as they seem in this teeming urban center, and Dickens reinforces this through each contrasting archetype. As the layers of this organic metropolis begin to unfold, the actual complexity of this unconventional giant of a character begins to emerge, and it is through mortality that Dickens chooses to disclose his prime paradoxes. Claudette Kemper Columbus asserts that eleven death scenes intensely punctuate the novel as a compulsory means of character/plot connectivity (611).[5] However, because each character is indicative of a larger social construct, these scenes are in actuality weightier commentary on the errors to be found within established conventions. Therefore, by examining each of the novel's major death scenes (and some lesser ones), it becomes clear that Dickens used these appositions to expose extraordinary cultural missteps.

In other words, although Dickens spends a great deal of time developing each well-defined social construct through appointed characters, the foibles of each social institution are so entrenched in its inner workings and locality that they are only truly exposed upon that character's death. Fatality, then, becomes the impetus for freeing the concealed dysfunctions of various social institutions. It is of great importance, then, that Dickens does not subject his most significant character to the rigid confines of the novel sphere— instead through Esther's parting words, the final words of the novel, "–even supposing— " (817), he allows for the continued expansion of the vast metropolis and its many communal façades. The sheer vulnerability of this final statement provides no true closure, and once again leaves behind the slightly uncomfortable impression that the City will continue to expand, shift, and contradict itself physically and metaphorically for infinitude.

NOTES

1. Glennie's research is in relation to Modern and Postmodern cities, but he recognizes and discusses the influences of these social institutions within the cities before them.

2. Levine's work primarily focuses on the concept of "affordance" or the "range of potential actions" as they relate to narrative form. She asserts that the length of *Bleak House* was necessary in order to represent the interconnectedness of Dickens's cityscape, and assigns importance to this expansive process as a stepping stone for other complex narratives using social networks in film. In this essay, I use Levine's concept of globalized networks as a jumping off point for deeper commentary on the characters involved.

3. Remarks on Bentham's commentary on "fictions of the law" as it relates to *Bleak House* can also be found in Polloczek's essay "The Marginal, the Equitable, and the Unparalleled" in Section II., which deals specifically with equity of the law in Dickens's novels (457 – 462).

4. This "unfettered product" refers to the precarious practices of Money Lenders as alluded to by Dickens throughout *Bleak House*. In this instance, Mr. Smallweed holds Mr. George accountable for the full repayment of a loan without just cause (Ch. 34).

5. This paraphrase provides the origination for the concept of this essay. However, Kemper Columbus's main focus is on the connections of characters and plots via rhetorical conventions, such as various sounds of the letter "J." She also draws many detailed connections at a grammatical level.

WORKS CITED

Baumgarten, Murray. "Reading Dickens Writing London." *Partial Answers: Journal of Literature and the History of Ideas*, vol. 9, no. 2, 2011, pp. 219-231. *Project MUSE*, doi: 10.1353/pan.2011.0020.

Beaumont, Matthew. "Beginnings, Endings, Births, Deaths: Sterne, Dickens, and *Bleak House*." *Textual Practice*, vol. 26, no. 5, 2012, pp. 807-827. *Academic Search Premier*, doi: 10.1080/0950236X.2012.669402.

Ben-Merre, David. "Wish Fulfillment, Detection, and the Production of Knowledge in *Bleak House*." *Novel: A Forum on Fiction*, vol. 44, no. 1, 2011, pp. 47-66. *JSTOR*, jstor.org/stable/41289226.

Columbus, Claudette Kemper. "The (Un)Lettered Ensemble: What Charley Does Not Learn About Writing in *Bleak House*." *Studies in English Literature 1500-1900 (Rice)*, vol. 28, no. 4, 1988, pp. 608. *Academic Search Premier*, doi:10.2307/450663.

Dickens, Charles. *Bleak House*, edited by Tatiana M. Holway, Barnes & Noble Classics, 2005.

Epstein, Amy Kallman. "Multifamily Dwellings and the Search for Respectability: Origins of the New York Apartment House." *Urbanism Past & Present*, vol. 5, no. 2 (10), 1980, pp. 29–39. *JSTOR*, jstor. org/stable/44403599.

Glennie, Paul. "Consumption, Consumerism and Urban Form: Historical Perspectives." *Urban Studies*, vol. 35, no. 5–6, May 1998, pp. 927–951. *JSTOR*, doi:10.1080/0042098984628.

Hale, Elizabeth. "Locations." *Esther's Narrative*, University of New England AU, 2014, esthersnarrative.une.edu.au/category/locations/.

Levine, Caroline. "Narrative Networks: *Bleak House* and the Affordances of Form." *Novel: A Forum on Fiction*, vol. 42, no. 3, 2009, pp. 517-523. *Academic Search Premier*, doi: 10.1215/00295132-2009-050.

Mangion, Carmen M. "Faith, Philanthropy and the Aged Poor in Nineteenth-Century England and Wales." *European Review of*

History, vol. 19, no. 4, 2012, pp. 515-530. *Academic Search Premier*, doi:10.1080/13507486.2012.697876.

Nolan, Meghan P. "The Socially Mobile Female in Victorian and Neo-Victorian Mysteries." *Transnational Crime Fiction Mobility, Borders and Detection*, edited by Maarit Piipponen et al., Springer International Publishing, 2020, pp. 135-152.

Polloczek, Dieter Paul. "The Marginal, the Equitable, and the Unparalleled: Lady Dedlock's Case in Dickens's *Bleak House*." *New Literary History*, vol. 30, no. 2, 1999, pp. 453-478. *Academic Search Premier*, doi:10.1353/nlh.1999.0029.

Steinlight, Emily. "Dickens's 'Supernumeraries' and the Biopolitical Imagination of Victorian Fiction." *Novel: A Forum on Fiction*, vol. 43, no. 2, 2010, pp. 227-250. *Academic Search Premier*, doi:10.1215/00295132-2010-002.

Stone, Marjorie. "Dickens, Bentham, and the Fictions of the Law: A Victorian Controversy and Its Consequences." *Victorian Studies*, vol. 29, no. 1, 1985, pp. 125-154. *JSTOR*, jstor.org/stable/3827568.

Taylor, Brooke D. "Spontaneous Combustion: When 'Fact' Confirms Feeling in *Bleak House*." *Dickens Quarterly*, vol. 27, no. 3, 2010, pp. 171-184. *Academic Search Premier*.

Upstate, Downstate and in His Dressing-gown: *The Mise en Abyme* of M. K. Lorens's Winston Marlow Sherman Series

Malcah Effron

"By day, he's a bulky, suede-elbowed Shakespeare professor. By night, he hunches over his typewriter and secretly becomes Henrietta Slocum—a mystery novelist renowned for her swanky Gilded Age snooper, G. Winchester Hyde."

Thus the paperback covers describe Winston Marlowe Sherman, the detective protagonist of M. K. Lorens's mystery series. M. K. Lorens, pseudonym for playwright and Early English scholar Lorraine Keilstrup, pulls from her background in academia and her background in the New York City theater scene in her five-novel mystery series published between 1990 and 1993 and set in the 1980s. The series features Sherman, an *emeritus* Shakespeare professor; Sarah Bernhardt Cromwell, his partner of forty years and a concert pianist; David Garrick Cromwell, Sarah's much younger brother and Royal Academy of Dramatic Arts (RADA) trained actor; Eddie Merriman, his friend and a retired Dickens professor; and Lloyd Agate, his former remedial writing student, who is police lieutenant in the small (fictional) Hudson Valley college town of Ainsley, New York. By centering the life of Ainsley around a (fictional) small liberal arts college Clinton College, and arts scenes—theater, classical music, and literature—in Manhattan, these novels confront the evolution of attitudes to the arts and humanities higher education in the United States from the 1950s to the 1980s. This critique appears amidst the metafictive collapsing of boundaries between art and life that occurs in detective novels with a detective novelist protagonist, contrasting the seeming chaos of reality with the controlled plotting of fiction.

As the detective protagonist is an English professor and mystery novelist by profession, all the narratives begin with crimes perpetrated against Sherman or his extended non-traditional family. Sometimes these cases refer to murders in Ainsley, New York, as in *Deception Island* (1990), in which the novel begins with the murder of a local Ainsley art dealer. Sometimes these cases refer to murders in New York City, as in the second novel, *Ropedancer's Fall* (1990), which begins with the death of a PBS program anchor in Manhattan. *Sweet Narcissus* (1990), the first novel of the series, establishes this upstate-downstate commuting nature of the series, opening with the narrative of an accidental death and theft of an Early Modern manuscript in Ainsley in the 1950s which are connected to a violent attack and subsequent murder in Manhattan the 1980s. The novels are thus neither wholly small-town cozies nor urban thrillers, but they wind the genres around each other to privilege the intrigue of the narrative and the cross-cultural experience of the upstate-downstate setting.

This double setting allows for two avenues of cultural commentary within the series: it uses the upstate college setting to comment on shifts in higher education in the United States, and it uses the Manhattan setting to comment on evolution in the arts in the United States, especially during the 1980s. In particular, these novels confront the commercialization of higher education and the shift to consumer-driven models of universities and arts, accompanied by the rise of middle management. Throughout the series, these ideas are implicitly addressed through an ongoing battle of wits between Sherman, a professor *emeritus* who has been pushed into a part-time teaching capacity, and the departmental and university administration trying to push him into full retirement. As a professor tenured in the 1950s, Sherman's complaints about pedagogical development might not always ring true with twenty-first century academic readers, but some of the issues are frighteningly familiar, more so because their appearance in these novels means they have decades-deep roots. These issues climax in the final novel of the series, *Sorrowheart* (1993), in which the main antagonist and murder victim is the new college chancellor who prioritizes university expansion at the expense of the town (18), student evaluations above all other evaluation criteria for instructors (56), grade inflation as a commercial strategy (57), and a massive rise in administrative positions with a corresponding cutting of faculty positions (59-60). The series even gives (very brief) acknowledgment of the change in the academic job market, when Sherman reflects that his refusal to retire contributes to "those waiting hordes of jobless Ph.D.s" (*Sweet* 172), calling out one of the largest issues in a system that commodifies jobs that many of its practitioners perceive as a *vocation* in the Catholic sense. The series situates higher education's shifting focus from education to commodification within the larger murder mystery narrative, arguing that the explicit commercialization of the arts and humanities in the 1980s is also criminal.

The critique of higher education flows from the detective protagonist's position as an academic; by making him a professor of literature whose partner is a concert pianist with whom he raises a RADA trained actor, the series creates space to address shifts in the arts more generally, especially because Ainsley is within a commutable proximity to New York City. The series works its way through different areas of arts under attack. *Sweet Narcissus* addresses commercialization of the performing arts — "a jiffy mix for success and quick fame" (90) — and *Ropedancer's Fall* critiques the commodification of literary publication and prizes: "We fed the plot lines, characters, all that crap, of the past ten Pulitzer Prize winners into our computers [so w]e knew we had a marketable product" (63). *Deception Island* addresses such commodification in the visual arts — "The syndicates were multiplying, buying up contract art — often of dubious quality — for their stockpiles" (23) — and *Dreamland* even addresses the mystery novel publishing market: "We're not so much people, or even writers, as products" (89). Taking a similar stance to the arts and humanities in the public sphere as in higher education, the series generally correlates social devaluation of these areas to the devaluation of human life that allows for murder.

However, the tone of these early 1990s novels frequently sounds elitist experienced from the present moment in the 2020s. Despite its self-promoted liberal attitudes toward women and sexuality—"Our [Sherman's and Sarah Cromwell's] unmarriage was [...] our way of thumbing our noses at the petty dictatorships of [the university and her father]" (27) — many of Sherman's critiques express white privilege, especially in a gatekeeping function that keeps non-WASPs out of elite institutions, as exemplified by the small town setting of Ainsley, New York. There is no (good) excuse for the unthinking attitudes toward Native Americans in these novels, with its dismissal of Navajo studies (170) plus its frequent references to the Lone Ranger and Tonto (101). Such examples of white elitism are clearly problematic, and, as scholars in the twenty-first century, *Mean Streets*'s current readership might additionally find it not only problematic but also surprising to see this elitism extend to a critique of popular fiction itself. Lorens marks the genre as unsuitable for academic study, calling collegiate courses in popular fiction "junk-food courses" (*Sweet* 26) introduced to appease a consumer-based model of higher education. In our current moment, it's (perhaps) hard to believe this was ever an objection with an abundance of such courses taught in universities around the world as well as academic journals devoted to the subject, of which *Mean Streets* is clearly one. Yet, when Lorens was writing these novels, popular fiction scholarship, and crime fiction scholarship in particular, had not yet experienced its present boom (*Clues: A Journal of Detection* first appeared only in 1980, as did Stephen Knight's foundational *Form and Ideology in Crime Fiction*; Kathleen Gregory Klein's *The Woman Detective: Gender & Genre* and Maureen Reddy's *Sisters in Crime: Feminism and the Crime Novel* aren't published until 1988). Thus, by keeping in mind the history of crime fiction scholarship and other evolutions in academic social norms, readers can contextualize the series, repudiating where needed, but appreciating what it does well.

For, though Sherman rejects the literary quality of popular genre classes (and many readers might recognize that others, including enrolled students, have shared the assumption that popular fiction classes won't require analytic work), Lorens's metafictional play shows the literary critical engagement in these "junk food" genres. With its layering of mystery narratives, mystery narrators, and mystery authors, the novels are subtly, yet wholly, metafictional experiments. When the first novel opens with the first-person narrator telling the reader "it was only natural for me to write the whole thing down [and] here's the way the story goes" (*Sweet* 4), the narrative suggests that the book in the reader's hand is going to be the first true-crime novel generated by a mystery fiction novelist. While the series moves in and out of its commitment to the idea of an autobiographical true-crime series, it never presents Henrietta Slocum as the author of these novels. Henrietta Slocum sticks to writing G. Winchester Hyde novels, even after an attempt to kill off Hyde at the end of *Sweet Narcissus*.

Part of the challenge of understanding the status of the relative narratives is the insistence of Eddie Merriman in calling Sherman "Hyde" when he dons his detective cap. Such moves encourage the explicit use of Hyde's detective strategies when Sherman investigates the murders he encounters in Ainsley and in New York City, echoing Harriet Vane in *Have His Carcase* (1932). Also similarly to Vane, Sherman (but perhaps not Slocum or Hyde) recognizes that the challenge of mystery detecting compared to mystery writing is that the author "was used to making up the clues as I needed them and changing them if they didn't work out" (*Sweet* 117). Yet, the series also demonstrates how the process of being a mystery writer, the process of being a mystery detective — and thus implicitly the process of being a mystery reader — can all feel functionally the same when things aren't going well (*Ropedancer's* 71). Such intricate weaving of the experience of the author, the detective, and the reader when faced with murder — fictitious or not — highlights the clever conversations between ontological planes and the way readers bring all experiences, both fictional and non-fictional, into the social construction of their own lived experiences. Such articulations likely will echo with mystery readers and reverberate in the minds of scholars interested in metafictional and other postmodern constructions.

Though a short, and perhaps much dated series, these novels still leave open many questions for the crime fiction analyst. Much work has been done on the detective figure in the detective novel as a comment on "the character of the writer" (Grauby 120) as Françoise Grauby does with Agatha Christie's Ariadne Oliver, or to study gender, as Sally Beresford-Sheridan does with Dorothy L. Sayers's Harriet Vane. Yet, these explorations usually function only in relation to these classical texts or otherwise privileging autobiographical inquiry, such as Ariadne Oliver or Harriet Vane as a way for Christie and Sayers, respectively to insert themselves into their novels (Grauby 116, 122; Pitt 172). With its layering of authorship, narration, and pseudonymity, M. K. Lorens's series offers an opportunity to investigate questions around authorship and gender, as her detective simultaneously occupies the roles of Professor Winston Sherman, novelist Henrietta Slocum, and (doubly) fictional detective G. Winchester Hyde. Though the series itself does not explicitly engage with these questions, it opens the door for mystery readers and scholars to ask what does it mean that Lorens's cis-male adopts a female pseudonym and writes about a cis-male (American) Gilded Age detective, with all the facetiousness (and related sexuality baggage) of a Hercule Poirot or a Peter Wimsey? What do we in this academic community make of calling an old-fashioned man Henrietta or the collapse of boundary between Sherman and Hyde as investigating detective protagonist? Do any of the answers we can generate to these questions continue to hold when faced with the androgynous pseudonym M. K. Lorens, an androgyny only somewhat mitigated by the author's photo included on the book jacket?

Outside the questions this novel series raises about gender, authorship, authority, and investigation, the author's attitude toward cultural changes is an opportunity for investigation into shifting values. The novel series discusses the changing values of arts and humanities in the United States in the second half of the twentieth century. Which of these fears are still validated in the twenty-first century and which fears have been outgrown? Which fears have had detrimental consequences and which fears were more indicative of inherent human conservativism? While none of these questions is answered by Sherman, his pseudonym Henrietta Slocum, or the pseudonymous M. K. Lorens, reading these novels with their multiple levels of textual realities can be a productive launching point for further investigation.

WORKS CITED

Beresford-Sheridan, Sally. "Bending the Genre: Portraying the Genders of Harriet Vane and Lord Peter Wimsey in the Detective Fiction of Dorothy L. Sayers." *CLUES: A Journal of Detection*, vol. 36, no. 2, 2018, pp. 19–28.

Grauby, Françoise. "'This Isn't a Detective Story, Mrs. Oliver': The Case of the Fictitious Author." *CLUES: A Journal of Detection*, vol. 34, no. 1, 2016, pp. 116-25.

Klein, Kathleen G. *The Woman Detective: Gender & Genre*. U of Illinois P, 1988.

Knight, Stephen. *Form and Ideology in Crime Fiction*. Macmillan, 1980.

Lorens, M. K. *Deception Island*. 1992. Bantam, 1993.

——. *Dreamland*. Bantam, 1990.

——. *Ropedancer's Fall*. Bantam, 1990.

——. *Sorrowheart*. 1993. Bantam, 1994.

——. *Sweet Narcissus*. 1990. Doubleday, 1993.

Pitt, Valerie. "Dorothy Sayers: The Predicaments of Women." *Literature and History*, vol. 14, no. 2, 1988, pp. 172-80.

Reddy, Maureen T. *Sisters in Crime: Feminism and the Crime Novel*. Continuum, 1988.

Sayers, Dorothy L. *Have His Carcase*. 1932. HarperCollins, 1995.

Detecting the South in Fiction, Film & Television

Deborah E. Barker and Theresa Starkey, editors
Louisiana State University Press, 2019 (350 pp.)

Detecting the South aims to reveal the often underestimated influence of the American South on detective fiction in print and screen. The Introduction harks back to the origins of detective fiction in the stories of Edgar Allan Poe, in particular his story set in New Orleans, "The Gold Bug." They note that Southern writers not known for crime fiction, including Mark Twain and William Faulkner, have contributed as well. *Detecting the South* chooses to see the South as an imaginary rather than a specific geographical area and examines the influence of that imaginary on the creation of detective fiction, while also exploring such issues as race, class, gender, sexual orientation, the environment, and social justice. Divided into four sections, the text's first section examines Southern Noir, while the other three sections discuss forms of detection.

In "Part I: *Detecting the South*," Megan Abbott and Ace Atkins, contemporary authors of crime and detective fiction, contribute essays in addition to those by academic scholars. Atkins explores the "noir landscape of the New South," and argues that crime fiction pushes the reader to look for the causes of society's problems. Bob Hodges examines Faulkner's novel *Sanctuary* (1931) and the 1933 film interpretation of it, *The Story of Temple Drake*, for Faulkner's creation of noir archetypes—the femme fatale, the villain (in this case the gangster) and the detective. Jacob Agner discusses rural settings that he dubs "mountainoir," with their "stigmatypes," or lower class characters considered "white trash." The New Orleans and Louisiana of authors Atkins and James Lee Burke, and of film and television, feature in the essays of Leigh Anne Duck and James A. Crank. Sarah Leventer also examines HBO's *True Detective* in her essay on Matthew McConaughey, while Susan Leonard covers suburban, domestic noir in its trajectory from *Desperate Housewives* to *Gone Girl*, seeing the latter as an intensification of tropes of the earlier series.

"Part II: Privately *Detecting the South*" focuses on detection by amateur and private detectives. Like Part I, Part II opens with essays by contemporary crime writers. Dominiqua Dickey writes of the creation of her Black character, Elnora May Hardin of Grenada, Mississippi, while Greg Herren describes the creation of Chanse MacLeod, the first gay male detective in New Orleans. Harriet Pollack examines the stories of Eudora Welty and the influence on her later work of her correspondence with Kenneth Millar, aka Ross Macdonald, with whom she established a life-long friendship after reviewing one of his novels. Claire Cothren analyzes Donna Tartt's *The Little Friend*, and its twelve-year old amateur detective, asserting that Tartt is more interested in leading the reader to reconsider stereotypes of the South than in solving the crime.

The television series *Yancy Derringer* is the subject of Phoebe Bronstein's essay, which argues that the show imagines the white patriarch as a rejection of the civil rights movement of the time, despite the diversity of the cast and the depiction of Derringer as a moderate. Kristopher Mecholsky's essay on John D. MacDonald sees MacDonald's crime fiction as an examination of the ecology and politics of Florida as an area doomed to suffer the consequences of humanity's impact on nature.

"Part III: Detecting Southern Cops" examines detection by detectives and police officers, beginning with Theresa Starkey's essay on *The Andy Griffith Show* (1960-68) and the whiteness of Sheriff Taylor and the fictional town of Mayberry. Contrary to most professional police, Taylor polices his town and its borders with a hefty dose of folk wisdom, common sense, and adherence to the golden rule as well as the law. Randall Wilhelm's essay on the film *One Foot in Eden* (2002) and the television series *Justified* (2010-2015) discusses Appalachian Noir. Yajaira M. Padilla studies the Latina detective of

Marcos McPeek Villatoro's *Home Killings* (2001); she is a southerner from Atlanta, based in Nashville, and a Latina in worlds typically divided into white and Black. Romilia Chacón's fluency in Spanish proves essential to the investigation. Gina Caison's essay probes the use of an attractive white female detective from Atlanta as "bait" and as a Southern presence in the New York squad room of *Law & Order: Special Victims Unit.*

The final section is "Part IV: Journalists Detecting the South." Riché Richardson examines the "detective journalism" of William Bradford Huie, who worked with Zora Neale Hurston. Jacqueline Pinkowitz investigates passing as Black, which she sees as a kind of detection, in the film version of *Black Like Me.* The collection closes with an essay by Zachary Vernon on contemporary journalists as "culture detectives," including famous writers such as V.S. Naipaul, writers not from the South, who claim to see and understand the "true South" based on whatever part of it they've experienced.

Detecting the South in Fiction, Film & Television is a well-organized critical anthology on an understudied region—a region so vast that no single volume can hope to encompass it. Aside from the challenge of cultural and geographical questions of identity, the study of printed texts and the visual texts of television and film itself presents many challenges. One can always note omissions—Carl Hiaasen of Florida, the Black author Attica Locke with her Black Texas Ranger, the Atlanta in L.A. of *The Closer*—but the anthology covers a lot of ground, and includes diverse voices. Barker and Starkey have created an admirable collection, which they hope will lead to other studies of Southern detective and crime fiction in print and visual texts.

—Linda Ledford-Miller
Professor Emerita of Spanish, Portuguese
and Literature of American Minorities
Department of World Languages and Cultures
University of Scranton

The Man of the Crowd: Edgar Allan Poe and the City

Scott Peeples with Photographs by Michelle Van Parys
Princeton University Press, 2020 (224 pp.)

In the introduction to his 2020 work *The Man of the Crowd: Edgar Allan Poe and the City*, Scott Peeples seeks to countermand the popular image of Edgar Allan Poe as a rootless, solitary figure. He endeavors to show Poe as a product of both his time and his physical environment, while including some cursory references to the works created at various places and stages in his life. Peeples organizes the book chronologically to highlight Poe's development as a writer and critic, as well as his alcoholism, his inability to keep a job, and his constant borrowing, in its five chapters: Richmond (1809-1827), Baltimore (1827-1838), Philadelphia (1838-1844), New York (1844-1848), and In Transit (1848-1849).

Peeples begins by placing Poe as distinct among his literary compatriots who were predominantly associated with a single locale they had been lifelong residents of or closely identified with: Hawthorne's New England environs, Stowe in Connecticut, Emerson and Thoreau in Concord, Whitman and Melville in New York City, etc. Peeples states that his goal is to show how Poe fit into his environment, creating "a compact biography of Poe that reconsiders his work and career in light of his itinerancy and his relationships to the cities where he lived" (5). This work traces the development of his career and his writing style as he became the familiar figure of literature, with his published explorations of the macabre echoing his alcoholism and personal tragedies.

This work offers a view of Poe as fairly hapless, buffeted by the consequences of his actions but helpless against his own character flaws of self-pity, self-aggrandizement, and self-centeredness as seen in his plans to marry two different women after his wife's death. This also serves to counter popular images of a heartbroken Poe drinking himself to death after the loss of his wife, a first cousin thirteen years his junior.

Peeples can lose the reader when connecting events throughout Poe's life, such as the deaths of his brother and foster father. A timeline of happenings in Poe's life at the front or back of the book would be helpful for the reader to clarify when Peeples is referencing people who had already died or left Poe's circle. This book would be appreciated by an audience that has had some exposure to Poe's works; with little in the way of literary criticism, it serves to provide some context for Poe's life and show how he fit (or did not, as was usually the case) into society. One interesting fact Peeples includes is that Poe's Philadelphia landlord from 1842-1843 was Michel Bouvier, great-great-grandfather of Jacqueline Kennedy Onassis. Peeples also expands the reader's preconceived notions of Poe's style and substance by referencing some of his lesser-known writings, such as multiple diatribes regarding the superiority of treated wooden pavement over stone.

The Man of the Crowd presents Poe as a product of the tragedies in his life, some of them exacerbated by his own actions. This text would be appreciated by Poe fans who want more context for Poe's works in the events of his life and development as a writer. It is also of interest to fans of American history leading up to the Civil War. It links the history and development of four eastern cities with the growth of one of America's most popular authors. Peeples occasionally mentions frequent themes in Poe's works, which encourages the casual reader to find less popular stories that feature familiar motifs.

Poe portrays the city in his detective fiction as a place of sinister strangers, where crimes are likely to occur. According to Peeples, when writing his detective fiction, Poe relied on newspaper accounts of real-life deaths, turning the New York City death of Mary Cecilia Rogers, likely from a botched abortion, into "The Mystery of Marie Rogêt." Peeples links the rise of newspapers, which allowed readers to puzzle over the details of grisly cases, to the burgeoning popularity of detective fiction. By fictionalizing contemporary crimes and offering his own solutions, Poe tapped into an audience that was eager to solve the gruesome puzzles happening around them.

The photography by Van Parys includes several photographs that overlay Poe's former residences on their contemporary surroundings. This helps not only to situate Poe as a product of his time, but also to highlight his continued legacy, as several of the houses were not places of long residence, though they are popular places for modern visitors.

This compact work including endnotes and the index is a quick read, enabling a wide audience to track Poe through four American cities and understand how his environment had an impact on his writing, his livelihood, and his personal life. Peeples demonstrates the rise and fall of Poe's literary ambitions as his goal to develop his own magazine was disrupted by his drinking, his problems with money, his impatience with lesser minds, and his need for affection. Ultimately, the tragedy of his death, cause still unknown, cuts short a prolific career that developed the modern detective fiction genre and popularized the horror genre. Peeples's work provides a concise biography of Poe and his evolution through his interactions with the people and culture of his chosen cities.

—Monica Lott
Composition Instructor
Kent State University-Geauga Campus

Contributors

Joydeep Bhattacharyya did his Bachelor of Arts in English Literature at Sri Aurobindo College, affiliated to the University of Delhi, India, and Master of Arts in English Literature at Jamia Millia Islamia (University), New Delhi. He holds an MPhil degree in Comparative Indian Literature from the Department of Modern Indian Languages and Literary Studies, an integral part of the University of Delhi. His area of specialization is detective fiction, with a special focus on British and Bengali detective fiction. Apart from his area of specialization, his fields of interest include postcolonial studies, popular culture, and translation studies. He has presented research papers at national and international conferences held at universities and venues across India. He has also contributed chapters in academic books in India and is currently working on another international research paper. He began teaching at Sri Guru Gobind Singh College of Commerce, affiliated with the University of Delhi, in January 2020.

Antoine Dechêne holds a PhD from the Université de Liège, Belgium. Most notably, he is the author of *Detective Fiction and the Problem of Knowledge* (Palgrave MacMillan, 2018) and the co-editor with Michel Delville of the first volume dedicated to the metaphysical thriller in French: *Le Thriller métaphysique d'Edgar Allan Poe à nos jours* (Presses Universitaires de Liège, 2016).

Malcah Effron is a Lecturer II in Writing, Rhetoric, and Professional Communication in the Department of Comparative Media Studies at MIT. She holds degrees from Washington University in St. Louis (A.B. English and Mathematics, 2004), the University of Chicago (M.A. Humanities, 2005), and Newcastle University in England (Ph.D. English Literature, 2010). Her research in crime fiction focuses on the narrative aspects, particularly the genre's frequent metafictional play with the borders of fictionality and reality and the consequences of such play upon social constructions of reality. Her peer-reviewed work appears in journals such as published articles in *The Journal of Narrative Theory*, *Narrative*, and *Women & Language*. She also edited *Function of Evil across Disciplines* (with Brian Johnson, Lexington Books, 2017) and *The Millennial Detective* (McFarland, 2011) and has contributed chapters to it as well as to *History of American Crime Fiction* (Cambridge, 2017) and *Teaching Crime Fiction* (2018). She has also served as a book reviewer for *Cercles*. She is a peer reviewer for *The Journal of Popular Culture* and *Crime Fiction Studies* and is on the *Mean Streets* editorial board. With Nicole Kenley, she is editing a special issue on space, place, and the detective narrative for *The Journal of Popular Culture* (volume 54, 2021). She is also the co-founder of the international Crime Studies Network (CSN).

Alexander N. Howe is a Professor of English and chair of the Division of Arts and Humanities at the University of the District of Columbia, where he offers courses on American literature, literary theory, and film. His research interests include crime and detective fiction, science fiction and film, and psychoanalysis. His recent publications include articles on the history of American crime fiction, female investigators in the works of Raymond Chandler, the pseudonymous thrillers of Louisa May Alcott, the disavowal of the body in AMC's *The Walking Dead*, and gender and posthumanism in Netflix's *Altered Carbon*. He is the author of *It Didn't Mean Anything: A Psychoanalytic American Detective Fiction* (McFarland, 2008) and co-editor of *Marcia Muller and the Female Private Eye: Essays on the Novels That Defined a Subgenre* (McFarland, 2009). He is currently completing a manuscript on the intersections between dystopian and detective fiction.

Linda Ledford-Miller has a Masters in Comparative Literature from the Pennsylvania State University, and in Luso-Brazilian Literature and Comparative Literature from the University of Texas, Austin, specializing in Literature of the Americas. She has published widely on travel writing and women writers. An avid reader of mysteries, she has shifted focus to crime fiction, working on Robert Downey, Jr.'s interpretation of Sherlock Holmes, gender roles in the *In Death* series by American J.D. Robb, the village mysteries of Canadian Louise Penny, the philosophical Inspector Espinosa series by Brazilian Luis Alfredo Garcia-Roza, the medieval mysteries of Ellis Peters' Brother Cadfael, and the importance of food for the Italian detective Guido Brunetti in Donna Leon's Venetian series and Salvo Montalbano in the series by Sicilian Andrea Camilleri.

Monica Lott, Ph.D. is the writing tutor at the Kent State University-Geauga campus and teaches composition at the Kent State-Twinsburg campus. Her doctoral dissertation focused on the works of Detection Club writers with an emphasis on the themes of war, gender, and nostalgia in the works of Dorothy L. Sayers and Agatha Christie. She has been published in *Michael Chabon's America: Magical Words, Secret Worlds, and Sacred Spaces; Interdisciplinary Literary Studies*; and the *Steinbeck Review*.

Rebecca Martin, Ph.D. is Professor Emerita of English at Pace University in New York. In addition to her PhD, which focused on the eighteenth-century Gothic novel in England, she holds a graduate certificate in film studies from City University of New York Graduate Center. In her academic career she created and taught courses on a wide range of literatures, as well as film history, theory and melodrama. Her interest in crime writing focuses on the hardboiled tradition. She also pursues an interest in the juncture of haunting, the spectral and technology. She edited two books for Salem Press, *Critical Insights: Crime and Detective Fiction* (2013) and *Critical Insights-Film: Bonnie and Clyde* (2016). In addition, she is co-editor of a new journal, *Mean Streets: A Journal of American Crime and Detective Fiction* (Pace UP), and was guest editor of a special issue, "Crime Writing," for *The Human: A Journal of Literature and Culture* (2016). Her other published work in collections and journals includes essays on crime writing pedagogy, detective authors Sue Grafton and Marcia Muller, the Gothic novel, film noir and French Poetic Realism, and on Hitchcock's *Notorious* and *North by Northwest* and the Cold War. She now lives in New Orleans, which is another mystery.

Jennifer Nolan is Associate Professor of English at North Carolina State University. As a print culture scholar, Dr. Nolan's research situates literature within the cultural, historical, editorial, and visual contexts surrounding its publication, with particular emphasis on F. Scott Fitzgerald, the short story, and popular American magazines during the first half of the twentieth century. Her recent articles have appeared in *Book History* (the journal for the Society for the History of Authorship, Reading, and Publishing), *The Journal of Modern Periodical Studies, American Periodicals*, and *The F. Scott Fitzgerald Review*.

Meghan P. Nolan, MFA, MA, Ph.D. is an Assistant Professor of English and Director of the Writing Center at SUNY Rockland, where she teaches a wide range of Composition and Literature courses including an upper-level Mystery/ Detective Fiction course. Recently, Nolan analyzed the evolution of perceptions of social mobility for contemporary versions of Victorian women in detective fiction in relation to those characterizations of the day for a chapter in *Transnational Crime Fiction: Mobility, Borders, and Detection* (Palgrave, 2020). She also presented on women's roles in Victorian and Neo-Victorian mysteries at an international conference in Malaga, Spain, in 2019. She is a multigenre writer, who focuses on fragmented perceptions of self-hood, and she has written several academic articles exploring these concepts pedagogically as well, including "Multiplicity and the Student Writer: Embracing Creative Multigenre Identity Work in the Writing Classroom" in *Exquisite Corpse: Studio Art-Based Writing in the Academy* (Parlor Press, 2019) and "Reframing Writerly Identity with the Works of Fernando Pessoa and Other Modernist Poets" to be included in a forthcoming MLA publication. Nolan has edited many creative and academic journals over the years, and her essays have also appeared in *Persona Studies*, *Thread*, and *The 100 Greatest Detectives*.

Walter Raubicheck, Ph.D. is a professor of English at Pace University in New York, where he teaches American Literature, film, and college composition. He is the co-author of *Scripting Hitchcock* (2011) and co-editor of *Hitchcock's Rereleased Films* (1991), both with Walter Srebnick. He also edited *Hitchcock and the Cold War* (2019). He has published essays on a number of crime fiction authors, including Arthur Conan Doyle, Dorothy Sayers and G. K. Chesterton, as well as essays on American authors such as F. Scott Fitzgerald, T. S. Eliot, and Dashiell Hammett. He is currently the editor of *Lex Naturalis*, a journal of natural law, and co-editor of *Mean Streets*, a journal devoted to American crime fiction, both published by the Pace University Press.

Call for Papers

Third issue of *Mean Streets: A Journal of American Crime and Detective Fiction*

Topic: AMERICAN "GOLDEN AGE" MYSTERY AND DETECTIVE FICTION 1920-1945

Proposals: July 15, 2021
Final essays: December 1, 2021

The "Golden Age" of mystery and detective fiction is generally agreed upon as bounded by World War I and World War II. While the designation is widely applied to both British and American fiction of the period, it has most closely adhered to British fiction, perhaps because American crime writing in the period was sharply bifurcated between Classical and Hard-boiled writing. "It was in Britain that the clue-puzzle had its richest development," claims Stephen Wright. So, in what lay the contribution of American writers? Are there unique features in their offerings to the Classical detective narrative? Is there any cross-fertilization between Classical and Hard-boiled practices? Do the circumstances of American life and culture of the period produce qualities notably different from British narratives?

Some possible approaches:
- Interrogation of the question: Is there an American Golden Age?
- Thematic explorations
- Contemporary resurgence of Golden Age interest/popularity
- Contributions of particular American publishers to Golden Age popularity and/or rediscovery (e.g., Rue Morgue Press, Library of Congress Crime Classics)
- Juxtaposition of Classic and Hard-boiled fiction in the period
- Analysis of the critical receptions of American writers by British critics
- Analysis of leading Golden Age authors such as

Anthony Abbot	Stuart Palmer
Anne Austin	Zelda Popkin
Hugh Austin	Ellery Queen
Earl Derr Biggers	Patrick Quentin
Anthony Boucher	Virginia Rath
John Dickson Carr	Clayton Rawson
Clyde B. Clason	Mary Roberts Rinehart
Dorothy Cameron Disney	Mabel Seeley
Todd Downing	Rex Stout
Mignon Eberhart	Kay Cleaver Strahan
Erle Stanley Gardner	John Stephen Strange
Frances Noyes Hart	Phoebe Atwood Taylor
C. Daly King	Darwin Teilhet
Rufus King	S.S. Van Dine
Helen McCloy	Carolyn Wells

Abstracts of 250 words with proposed title should be directed no later than July 15, 2021, to the editors: Rebecca Martin (doc.rmartin@gmail.com) and Walter Raubicheck (wraubicheck@pace.edu).

Final papers of 7000-8000 words will be due by December 1, 2021, with publication anticipated in spring 2022. Feel free to send questions to both editors.

About *Mean Streets*

This journal is published by the Pace University Press (New York City), which has been sponsoring scholarly journals since the 1980s.

Mean Streets is a refereed journal edited by two scholars in literature and film and guided by an Editorial Board comprised of distinguished scholars from several disciplines. Submissions will be reviewed by the editors and selected Board members.

The journal's first issue appeared in spring 2020. Copies may be ordered at press.pace.edu/journals/mean-streets/.

The first volume of *Mean Streets: A Journal of American Crime and Detective Fiction*
was published in Spring 2021
by Pace University Press

Cover and Interior Layouts by Kelly Gomez
The journal was typeset in Minion Pro and Gandhi Serif
and printed by Lightning Source in La Vergne, Tennessee

Pace University Press

Director: Manuela Soares
Associate Director: Karen Holt
Design Consultant: Joseph Caserto

Graduate Assistants: Delaney Anderson and Kelly Gomez
Student Aide: Rachel Smithline

CPSIA information can be obtained
at www.ICGtesting.com
Printed in the USA
BVHW040509050921
615876BV00008B/152

9 781935 625636